WHEN DISSENTS MATTER

CONSTITUTIONALISM
AND DEMOCRACY

Gregg Ivers and
Kevin T. McGuire,
Editors

When Dissents Matter

JUDICIAL DIALOGUE THROUGH
US SUPREME COURT OPINIONS

Pamela C. Corley, Amy Steigerwalt,
and Artemus Ward

University of Virginia Press | Charlottesville and London

University of Virginia Press
© 2023 by the Rector and Visitors of the University of
Virginia
All rights reserved
Printed in the United States of America on acid-free
paper

First published 2023

ISBN 978-0-8139-5016-7 (hardcover)
ISBN 978-0-8139-5017-4 (paper)
ISBN 978-0-8139-5018-1 (ebook)

9 8 7 6 5 4 3 2 1

Library of Congress Cataloging-in-Publication data is
available for this title.

Cover art: Wangkun Jia/shutterstock.com

To Megan and Greg — PCC
To my chosen family. LYLC — AS
To my chosen family — AW

CONTENTS

ILLUSTRATIONS

Figures

Tables

ACKNOWLEDGMENTS

Many people helped to bring this project to fruition. We thank those who made available their data: James F. Spriggs II, Rachael Hinkle, and Michael Nelson. We wish to recognize and thank the discussants at various conferences over the years who provided us comments and constructive advice and suggestions: Lisa Holmes, Chris Tecklenburg, Jordan Carr Peterson, Morgan Hazelton, Matt Hall, Ryan Hubert, Susan Johnson, Benjamin Kassow, Rachel Schutte, Paul Collins, Lee Epstein, Justin Wedeking, Ryan Black, and Justin DePlato. Additionally, many thanks to the anonymous reviewers who gave their time to improve this work. Finally, thanks to Nadine Zimmerli for her support for this project.

Although this volume represents original research, chapter 3 is a revised version of "Intra-Court Dialogue: The Impact U.S. Supreme Court Dissents" (Corley and Ward 2020) that appeared in the *Journal of Law and Courts*.

WHEN DISSENTS MATTER

Introduction

A Theory of Judicial Dialogue and Dissent

IN 1977, THE Minnesota legislature enacted a statute limiting the types of containers milk could be sold in; paper nonreusable containers were allowed, but plastic nonreusable containers were prohibited (*Minnesota v. Clover Leaf Creamery Co.* 1981). The purpose of the act was to "promote resource conservation, ease solid waste disposal problems, and conserve energy" (459). However, opponents argued that the act "would merely increase costs of retail milk products and prolong the use of ecologically undesirable paperboard milk cartons" (460). Several Minnesota dairies and plastic manufacturers filed a lawsuit against the state.

The Minnesota District Court found the evidence regarding the probable consequences of the act to be in "'sharp conflict'" (460). The court ultimately resolved the conflict in favor of the dairies and plastic manufacturers, finding that the act would not succeed in realizing its stated purpose. Furthermore, the district court determined that the actual purpose of the act "'was to promote the economic interests of certain segments of the local dairy and pulpwood industries at the expense of the economic interests of other segments of the dairy industry and the plastics industry'" (460). In addition to relying on state law, the district court struck down the act based on the Fourteenth Amendment's substantive Due Process Clause and the Equal Protection Clause, as well as the Commerce Clause.

Minnesota appealed to the Supreme Court of Minnesota, which affirmed the lower court's decision. Contrary to the lower court, the Minnesota Supreme Court found that the purpose of the act was "'to promote the state interests of encouraging the reuse and recycling of materials and reducing the amount and type of material entering the solid waste stream,' and acknowledged the legitimacy of this purpose" (460–61). The Minnesota Supreme Court concluded, however, that there was not a rational relationship between the means chosen—discrimination against plastic, nonreusable containers—and the act's purpose (461).

The United States Supreme Court granted certiorari and reversed, upholding the statute.[1] According to the majority opinion, the parties agreed that the proper standard of review under the Equal Protection Clause was the rational basis test, and the Court accepted the Minnesota Supreme Court's finding regarding the purpose of the act (461–62). Thus, the Court stated that it was deciding "the narrow issue whether the legislative classification between plastic and nonplastic nonreturnable milk containers is rationally related to achievement of the statutory purposes" (463).

When reviewing legislation under the Equal Protection Clause, the Court stated that it must approve legislation "[w]here there was evidence before the legislature reasonably supporting the classification" (464). While evidence may exist for both sides of this particular debate about the best course of action, the Court noted that it is the legislature's job to determine the best policy option: "The Minnesota Supreme Court may be correct that the Act is not a sensible means of conserving energy. But we reiterate that 'it is up to legislatures, not courts, to decide on the wisdom and utility of legislation'" (469). Accordingly, the Court found that the Minnesota Supreme Court erred by "substitut[ing] its judgment for that of the legislature" (469).

Justice John Paul Stevens dissented, arguing that the majority opinion was "based upon a newly discovered principle of federal constitutional law," the principle that "the Federal Constitution defines not only the relationship between Congress and the federal courts, but also the relationship between state legislatures and state courts" (477). Justice Stevens took issue with the majority's assertion that "'it is not the function of the courts to substitute their evaluation of legislative facts for that of the legislature'" (470). According to Justice Stevens, although that assertion is correct regarding federal courts, "I know of nothing in the Federal Constitution that prohibits a State from giving lawmaking power to its courts. Nor is there anything in the Federal Constitution that prevents a state court from reviewing factual determinations made by a state legislature or any other state agency" (479–80). Justice Stevens argued instead that

> the factual considerations drawn by the Minnesota courts concerning the deliberation of the Minnesota Legislature are entitled to just as much deference as if they had been drafted by the state legislature itself and incorporated in a preamble to the state statute. The State of Minnesota has told us in unambiguous language that this statute is not rationally related to any environmental objective; it seems to me to be a matter of indifference, for purposes of applying the federal Equal Protection Clause, whether that message to us from the State of Minne-

sota is conveyed by the State Supreme Court, or by the state legislature itself. (481–82)

The majority opinion specifically responded to Justice Stevens's dissent:

JUSTICE STEVENS' dissenting opinion argues that the Minnesota Supreme Court, when reviewing a challenge to a Minnesota statute on equal protection grounds, is not bound by the limits applicable to federal courts, but may independently reach conclusions contrary to those of the legislature concerning legislative facts bearing on the wisdom or utility of the legislation. This argument, though novel, is without merit. A state court may, of course, apply a more stringent standard of review as a matter of state law under the State's equivalent to the Equal Protection or Due Process Clauses. And as the dissent correctly notes, *post* at 479–481, the States are free to allocate the lawmaking function to whatever branch of state government they may choose. But when a state court reviews state legislation challenged as violative of the Fourteenth Amendment, it is not free to impose greater restrictions as a matter of federal constitutional law than this Court has imposed. [citations omitted]

The majority continued:

The standard of review under equal protection rationality analysis — without regard to which branch of the state government has made the legislative judgment — is governed by federal constitutional law, and a state court's application of that standard is fully reviewable in this Court on writ of certiorari. JUSTICE STEVENS concedes the flaw in his argument when he admits that "a state court's decision invalidating state legislation on federal constitutional grounds may be reversed by this Court if the state court misinterpreted the relevant federal constitutional standard." *Post* at 489. (462n6)

Justice Stevens criticized the majority's opinion on another point: "I find it extraordinary that this federal tribunal feels free to conduct its own *de novo* review of a state legislative record in search of a rational basis that the highest court of the State has expressly rejected. There is no precedent in this Court's decisions for such federal oversight of a State's lawmaking process" (482).

The majority again responded: "And contrary to his argument that today's judgment finds 'no precedent in this Court's decisions,' *post* at 482, we have frequently reversed State Supreme Court decisions invalidating state statutes or local ordinances on the basis of equal protection analysis more stringent than that sanctioned by this Court. Never have we suggested that our review of the judgments in such cases differs in any relevant respect because they were reached by state courts, rather than federal courts" (462fn6) [citations omitted].

In response, Justice Stevens added the following footnote to his dissent:

> In its footnote 6, *ante* at 461–463, the Court takes issue with my suggestion that its action in this case is unprecedented by citing four cases in which the Court reversed State Supreme Court decisions invalidating provisions of state law on federal equal protection grounds. See *Idaho Dept. of Employment v. Smith,* 434 U.S. 100 (1977) (per curiam); *Arlington County Board v. Richards,* 434 U.S. 5 (1977) (per curiam); *Richardson v. Ramirez,* 418 U.S. 24 (1974); *Lehnhausen v. Lake Shore Auto Parts,* 410 U.S. 356 (1973). In each of those cases, however, this Court concluded that the state court had applied an incorrect legal standard; in none did this Court reassess the factual predicate for the state court decision. (482n7)

Justice Stevens's footnote continued by discussing those cases in detail, concluding:

> As I read the cases cited by the majority, they are simply inapposite in this case. My own research has uncovered no instance in which the Court has reversed the decision of the highest court of a State, as it does in this case, because the state court exceeded some federal constitutional limitation upon its power to review the factual determinations of the state legislature. The Court has never before, to my knowledge, undertaken to define, as a matter of federal law, the appropriate relationship between a state court and a state legislature. (484n7).

The majority, once again responding to Justice Stevens's dissenting arguments, concluded in its footnote 6, stating that "JUSTICE STEVENS' argument in the dissenting opinion that today's treatment of the instant case is extraordinary and unprecedented, see *post* at 482, and n. 7, is simply wrong" (462n6).

This back and forth between the majority opinion and the dissent illustrates the internal yet public debate that can occur on the Supreme Court between the majority coalition and the dissenting coalition. What was it about Justice Stevens's dissent that provoked the majority into responding? Why did the majority opinion coalition feel compelled to respond to the specific arguments Justice Stevens made, even including additional Supreme Court precedent in the majority opinion? In the same case, Justice Lewis Powell wrote a separate opinion concurring and dissenting in part from the majority, declining to join the Court's holding with respect to the Commerce Clause. The majority did not address Justice Powell's opinion, rather leaving it to stand on its own. Why did the justices in the majority believe the best course of action was to draw additional attention to Justice Stevens's arguments, rather than simply ignoring them as they did Justice Powell's?

We argue in this book that the justices are engaged, like other actors in the national policymaking process, in a debate over law and policy. And, as in any debate or dialogue, there are sometimes disagreements among the multiple parties. These internal disagreements on the Court may become public when a justice decides to dissent from the Court's decision. When this disagreement enters the public realm through the various dissenting opinions of the justices, the majority must determine whether to respond to the opposing arguments or let them lie fallow. Future majorities must similarly decide whether to reference dissents from past cases. We argue that a contemporaneous majority will bring the justices' internal dialogue into the formal record of the majority opinion when a dissent poses a particular threat to the strength and position of the majority opinion. In *Minnesota v. Clover Leaf Creamery Co.*, the majority clearly felt Justice Stevens's attacks posed a particular danger to the strength of the majority's position, and did so in a way Justice Powell's opposing arguments did not. And, to fully defend its position, the majority determined a strong response to Justice Stevens's dissent was the best option. We propose that future Court majorities engage in a different calculation, including past dissents they believe will aid their arguments. We offer in this chapter our theory of when and why such calculations are most likely to occur, and then test this theory in our succeeding empirical chapters.

It's a Dialogue, Not a Soliloquy

The process of policymaking is complex and multifaceted. It involves a multitude of actors, a variety of decision points, and generally stretches out over decades. Basic American politics courses teach that the US government is composed of three branches: the executive, the legislative, and the judicial. The third branch of government, however, is many times overlooked in the discussion of how policy is created, implemented, and altered over time. Although Robert Dahl argued in 1957 that the United States Supreme Court was a primary actor in the national policymaking alliance, scholars, pundits, and laypersons alike continue to ignore the courts' role in the policymaking process. Making policy is not, however, simply the process of drafting and enacting legislation. Making policy also involves implementation by executive branch actors and the public, as well as interpretation and clarification by the courts.

An important part of the policymaking process is a dialogue regarding law and policy.[2] We use the term "dialogue" to refer to an ongoing, dynamic conversation about what the law is and what it should be. Law itself develops incrementally over time, reflecting a combination of statutes, rules, regulations, judicial decisions, and broader policy debates. The participants in this legal and policy dialogue are concerned with determining their policy positions and making decisions; at the same time, they are also focused on explaining their views to others with the goal of persuasion. Decisions are made at certain time points, but the larger debate itself continues as policies and issues, and the law writ large, constantly evolve, and participants both enter and leave the conversation.

The courts, and especially the justices of the United States Supreme Court, play a central role in this discourse. "The dialogue that takes place among the justices is a reflection of a far larger dialogue taking place among the citizenry" (Urofsky 2017, xiii). The justices in each case work to interpret both the United States Constitution as well as acts of Congress and statutes enacted by state legislatures. Additionally, the justices, through their decisions, clarify important components of legal doctrines (see, e.g., Corley, Steigerwalt, and Ward 2013). Justices, and other judges, engage in this policymaking dialogue every time they decide a case. In each and every case, the justices are asked to interpret and apply the laws on the books, and to decide what these laws actually mean and how they apply to particular situations. These decisions are not the end of the conversation, however, but rather another entry in this ongoing discussion. Scholars have demonstrated "that courts are inextricably entwined with the rest of the policy process" whereby "policy outcomes at any given point are likely to be the result of a long-running set of political conflicts taking place across multiple institutions" (Keck 2014, 203; see also

Shapiro 1964; Burgess 1992; Devins 1996; Barnes and Miller 2004; Pickerill 2004; Silverstein 2009; Blackstone 2013).

We expand on the conception of a "constitutional dialogue" offered by Melvin I. Urofsky (2017) to argue that the dialogue justices are engaged in goes well beyond just discussions about the Constitution to encompass the whole of the legal and policy discussion happening across the United States, and thus, we include both constitutional *and* statutory law. Including the Court's statutory decisions in our theoretical framework not only ensures we capture the entirety of the Court's work, but also illuminates the important ways in which the Court's role in the national policymaking debate can influence multiple actors outside the Court. The statutory cases the Supreme Court hears are no less important and wide-reaching than those addressing constitutional questions, and, in fact, an argument can even be made that the Court's most direct and ongoing influence on the legal and policy debate happens within the statutory realm, as the implementation and interpretation of laws occur continuously. The Court is routinely asked to clarify interpretations of statutory law, and those interpretations can be the impetus for important changes to federal laws, ranging from the expansion of when a paycheck discrimination suit can be filed (responding to the Court's decision in *Ledbetter v. Goodyear Tire* 2007) to including expert witness fees in the definition of "reasonable attorney's fees" in civil rights cases (responding to the Court's decision in *West Virginia University Hospitals v. Casey* 1991). While these statutory cases may not be as "sexy" as constitutional cases addressing issues such as abortion and affirmative action, they are many times the decisions that more clearly affect both the broader policy conversation as well as the day-to-day activities of the American people.

We argue that the justices' contribution to this legal and policy dialogue has both an external and an internal component. First, the justices in each case are engaging in a discussion with each of the other actors in the national policymaking process, whether that be members of the legislative and executive branches, lower court judges, lawyers, potential litigants, or the public. Second, the justices participate in a conversation among themselves, as they discuss and debate how best to understand, interpret, and apply sections of the Constitution, statutory provisions, and their past precedents. The justices' dialogue, whether internal or external, is dynamic and ongoing, directed both at their contemporaries as well as future actors in the policymaking process.

The justices engage in this discourse publicly through their written opinions. While we know that extensive conversations and discussions occur between the justices during Conference sessions, between chambers, and through the opinion-writing process, our contemporaneous insights come only through the justices' opinions. And, perhaps more importantly, it is only these written opinions that officially contribute to the broader policy and legal debate with other actors and the public.

The United States' adoption of the common law system means that the written opinions released by the Supreme Court serve as the only official mode of communication between the justices and those outside the Court. Why? Because the opinion itself is the explanation, and the sum total of the explanation. As Justice William Brennan once explained:

> A great Chief Justice of my home State [of New Jersey] was asked by a reporter to tell him what was meant by a passage in an opinion which had excited much lay comment. Replied the Chief Justice, "Sir, we write opinions, we don't explain them." This wasn't arrogance — it was his picturesque, if blunt, way of reminding the reporter that the reasons behind the social policy fostering an independent judiciary also require that the opinions by which judges support decisions must stand on their own merits without embellishment or comment from the judges who write or join them. (Brennan 1959)

The result is that the language used by the justices is important and, consequently, the justices spend considerable time crafting their opinions. Members of the executive and legislative branch, lower court judges, and the public in turn spend substantial time reading these opinions, both now and in the future.

An important component of this dialogue, both internal and external, is the use of dissents. A dissent by a justice is a public expression of disagreement with the outcome and reasoning of the majority opinion. Justices do not dissent lightly. As Justice Harlan Fiske Stone explained to then-Harvard Law Professor Felix Frankfurter in 1928:

> I always write a dissent with real reluctance and often acquiesce in opinions with which I do not fully agree, so you may know how strongly I have really felt in order to participate in so many dissents as I have recently. But where a prevailing view rests upon what appear to me to be false economic notions, or upon reasoning and analogies which will not bear analysis, I think great service is done with respect to the future

development of the law, in pointing out fallacies on which the prevailing view appears to rest even though the particular ruling made should never be overruled. (quoted in Mason 1956, 260–61)

Dissents send a strong, public signal that a justice believes her colleagues decided the case incorrectly. Dissents illustrate that there is more than one side to an issue, that reasonable people disagree, that issues are difficult, and that "fissures [exist] in the broader society" (Urofsky 2017, xiii). And dissents spell out where these fissures exist and exactly how the justice would decide the case differently.

A dissenting opinion is not law like the majority opinion is; it does not bind the litigants and it has no precedential value. However, dissents do potentially influence the strength of the Court's opinion and its broader standing in the nation. Judge Learned Hand opined that any disagreement over the majority opinion "cancels the impact of monolithic solidarity on which the authority of a bench of judges so largely depends" (Hand 1958, 72). James R. Zink, James F. Spriggs III, and John T. Scott (2009) find that the public is less likely to agree with and accept non-unanimous decisions; thus, there does appear to be some empirical support for the claim that dissents undercut the majority opinion.

In the early days of the Republic, the Supreme Court was known for the practice of acquiescence whereby justices would express their disagreement with the majority view during Conference but then join the ultimate, unanimous final opinion. The result was a public show of unity to bolster the legitimacy of the Court that hid private discord. Over time, however, as we discuss more fully in chapter 1, Supreme Court justices increasingly favored the individual expression of dissent. But, even as dissent has become more commonplace, the modern-day Court has still worked to suppress dissents in certain cases. In *Brown v. Board of Education* (1954)—holding racial segregation in public schools unconstitutional—Chief Justice Earl Warren "wanted a single, unequivocating opinion that could leave no doubt that the Court had put Jim Crow to the sword" (Kluger 1977, 683). Scholars routinely suggest that the unanimity Chief Justice Warren secured helped insulate *Brown* against subsequent challenges. For example, Kevin H. Smith (2005, 118) argues, "*Brown's* core holding was never subjected to serious challenges. A unanimous Supreme Court decision saw to that."

Alternatively, a number of justices in the modern era have argued that dissents are a necessary part of the Court's decision-making process and may even bolster the strength of the majority opinion and the Court's legitimacy. In contrast to majority opinions that are accompanied by a dissent, unanimous opinions may be the result of compromise, masking genuine disagreement, and potentially watering down or weakening the arguments in the majority opinion (Corley, Steigerwalt, and Ward 2013). In fact, one Supreme Court justice suggested that unanimity came at a price in *Brown:* "The cost was having 'all deliberate speed' come in. I think it would have been better to have the dissent spelled out . . . have the dissenters tell their problems, and then have a strong opinion to answer the dissent rather than coming down with a weak opinion so that everyone would sign. I think it is better to acknowledge what argument there is on a controversial issue like that" (Perry 1991, 148). Scholars indeed find that the public airing of dissent can lead to increased public acceptance of the Court's decision, particularly in low-salience cases, as dissents provide evidence of a fair, deliberative process (Salamone 2014).

Dissents can thus serve to strengthen majority opinions, and even potentially the degree to which the majority opinion is publicly accepted, by raising serious objections that the majority must answer. The result in such a situation is a majority opinion more forceful and perhaps more persuasive to lower courts, litigants, and the larger polity. Justice Brennan argued that dissents force majority opinion writers to deal with the hardest questions and keep the majority accountable for the rationale of its decisions (Brennan 1986). And Justice Ruth Bader Ginsburg noted that "there is nothing better than an impressive dissent to lead the author of the majority opinion to refine and clarify her initial circulation," describing this phenomenon as the "in-house impact" (Ginsburg 2010, 3). In other words, dissenting opinions can have an immediate impact, contributing to the law's development and arguably helping to improve the majority opinion.

And, finally, recent justices argue for the airing of disagreement to bolster the ongoing legal and policy debate that will continue into the future. The legal issues that come before the Court today have many times been heard by past Courts and will likely be heard by future Courts as well. Justice Antonin Scalia noted, "When history demonstrates that one of the Court's decisions has been a truly horrendous mistake, it is comforting—and conducive of respect for the Court—to look back and realize that at least some of the justices saw the danger and gave voice, often eloquent voice, to their concern" (Scalia 1998, 19).

But not all dissents are created equal, and not all dissents contribute similarly to the ongoing legal and policy dialogue. In some instances, the majority continues the discussion by responding to the dissent in the majority opinion. This back-and-forth between the majority and the dissent highlights for the public, and the other actors in the policymaking dialogue, that this is an issue of continuing debate and deliberation. And, as many justices have suggested, dissents can result in a stronger majority opinion. In other cases, however, the majority simply ignores the dissent, putting an end to the justices' internal dialogue. Why? What distinguishes those dissents where the majority wants to respond—or feels it must respond—from those where the Court determines the proper response is no response at all?

Additionally, why are certain dissents cited by majority opinions in the future while others are not? According to Justice Scalia: "Unlike majority opinions, [dissents] need not be read after the date of their issuance. They will not be cited, and will not be remembered, unless some quality of thought or of expression commends them to later generations" (Scalia 1998, 23). Which dissents are cited by future Courts, thus suggesting they displayed the necessary quality of thought or expression needed to be recalled and then deliberately revived in the continuing dialogue?

In this book, we examine why some dissents contribute to the ongoing discussion while others are consigned to the proverbial dustbin of history. In the next sections, we lay out a comprehensive theory of dissents that addresses not only why justices dissent and how they do so, but also, more importantly, when their colleagues will feel most compelled to include the dissent in the majority opinion, thereby continuing the debate.

Motivations for Dissent

At their core, dissents express disagreement. Specifically, dissents reflect the debates the justices have—just like those in the executive and legislative branches and public have—over law and policy. And dissents announce to the world that a justice disagrees with her colleagues. As Justice Oliver Wendell Holmes Jr. once stated, "I am unable to agree with the judgement of the majority of the Court, and although I think it useless and undesirable, as a rule, to express dissent, I feel bound to do so in this case and to give my reasons for it." Justices thus dissent when they believe their colleagues are grievously wrong and the cost of staying silent is greater than the potential cost of speaking out (see, e.g., Ginsburg 2010).

While dissent on the Supreme Court has grown more commonplace over time, dissents are still viewed as a last resort. Justice Louis Brandeis proclaimed, "It is more important that the applicable rule of law be settled than it be settled right"; he further argued in favor of joining even disagreeable decisions for the purposes of ensuring legal clarity from the Court (Brandeis, J., dissenting, *Burnet v. Coronado Oil & Gas Co.* 1932). Early years on the Court showcased this belief, as justices routinely acquiesced and joined the majority to present a united front to the country when final decisions were released (see, e.g., Epstein, Segal, and Spaeth 2001).

What changed, leading justices to now routinely argue that dissent is necessary, if not required, when disagreement arises? In previous work (Corley, Steigerwalt, and Ward 2013), we argue that the Court's shift from the norm of acquiescence to a culture of dissensus can be traced to what we term the Roosevelt Court (1937–47) and the rise of an individualized, academic-style environment on the Court. Not only did the Roosevelt Court justices, including Chief Justice Harlan Stone, support the airing of disagreements, but institutional norms and processes shifted as well. Conference discussion expanded, calls for case re-argument increased, and the opinion-writing process became longer and more fraught. Following the Roosevelt Court era, the Court implemented a number of important institutional and procedural changes over the decades, each of which aided dissent in flourishing: the adoption of the discretionary docket, the addition of the case syllabus, and the formalization of dissent assignments, to name a few. We provide a more comprehensive historical overview in chapter 1 of these institutional and procedural changes. Most important, our argument is that the shift toward a norm of dissensus is not merely a function of certain justices joining the Court, but rather that the implementation of these structural changes enabling, if not encouraging, dissent makes a return to the norm of consensus virtually impossible.

But what do justices hope to accomplish when they dissent? Dissents do not establish law nor do they provide guidance to lower courts or external actors. And, as we show in chapters 4 and 5, most dissents are ignored by both contemporaneous and future Courts. Thus, why do justices feel the need to make these disagreements public?

One key motivation for dissent is precisely to announce publicly the existence and reasoning for disagreement, and to enshrine it in the public record. Justice Brennan (1986, 430) maintained that dissents safeguard the integrity of the judicial decision-making process, because dissents keep the majority accountable for the rationale and consequences of its decisions. Dissents not only direct attention to difficulties with the majority's decision, but also contribute to the marketplace of competing ideas (Brennan 1986, 430). Furthermore, if there were no dissents, justices in the future could only consider the majority's reasons for its judgment instead of having access to previous conversations between the justices (Stack 1996). Dissents allow the majority's reasoning to continue being evaluated over time: "Each time the Court revisits an issue, the justices are forced by a dissent to reconsider the fundamental questions and to rethink the results" (Brennan 1986, 436). Dissents thus provide an outlet for justices to express fundamental disagreements, and ensure they are recorded for posterity.

Justices may also pursue several additional goals when they dissent. First, a dissenting justice wants to persuade her colleagues that they are wrong, and to instead adopt the reasoning and decision advocated in the dissent. Writing a dissent offers a mechanism to exert leverage in the dissenter's bargaining and negotiating with the majority coalition. Prior to any opinions being formally released, they are circulated around the Court. Majority opinion authors draft the first iteration of the majority opinion, and then await responses from their colleagues (see, e.g., Maltzman, Spriggs, and Wahlbeck 2000). Some justices may respond by signing on the opinion as drafted; some may ask the majority opinion writer for changes, additions, or deletions; and some may decide to draft a separate opinion that they will similarly circulate among their colleagues. The majority opinion author must then decide whether to make the requested changes—whether they be small edits or substantial changes to the proposed holding—to try to appease both members of the majority coalition as well as those who have expressed clear disagreement.

Potential dissenting justices know their colleagues wish to stave off dissents (and concurrences) if at all possible. In an ideal world, a justice will draft a dissent, and her colleagues will recognize their folly and adopt the dissenter's argument. Research based on the justices' papers reveals that such instances occur, though fairly infrequently. One such example we know of occurred in *Martin v. Struthers* (1943), a case that struck down a law prohibiting Jehovah's Witnesses from distributing pamphlets by going door to door. Justices Harlan Stone and Frank Murphy both circulated dissents in response to Justice Hugo Black's draft majority opinion. Based on the arguments of these dissents, Justice Black changed his mind, and the ideas expressed in the initial draft dissents eventually formed the holding of the majority decision (Urofsky 2017, 16).

More common is that the majority may narrow its opinion or move it somewhat toward the dissenting position, with the hopes that the potential dissenter will be willing to abandon her position in favor of the proposed compromise position. Consider Justice Powell's discussion with his clerk Phil Jordan concerning Powell's dissent in *Franks v. Bowman* (1976). Justice Powell explained to Jordan: "the role of a dissenter is similar to that of an advocate. . . . [W]here there is room for rational doubt, we should resolve it strongly in favor of our position."[3] After Justice Powell circulated his dissent, Justice Brennan—the majority opinion author—responded: "I am making a few small revisions in light of Lewis' most recent circulation. I must say Lewis seems to have made a full scale retreat from his original position. . . . Thus our opinions don't seem to differ to any great extent. I am making this clear in a new footnote."[4] Justice Powell replied, somewhat tongue-in-cheek, "If Bill really thinks there is no material difference, it would clarify the situation for everyone—and especially for the lower courts—if Bill were to join my opinion. He would be most welcome. Or, as an alternative, I cheerfully make my opinion available as a substitute for Part III and Part IV of his opinion. But in all candor, I view our opinions and positions as irreconcilable."[5] After Justice Brennan's fourth draft was circulated, Justice Powell noted on the draft: "At least we have Bill hopping! And he has made a stronger case for his view."[6] This back-and-forth exchange, which plays out via Conference deliberations, inter-chamber discussions, and the exchange of draft opinions, is a crucial component of how the justices debate law and policy. And the use of dissents as bargaining tools is a key mechanism of negotiation to persuade a fellow justice or group of justices to adopt another's favored position.

Similarly, dissenting justices may also be cognizant that while they have lost the immediate battle, they may win the ultimate war by influencing their colleagues, or even future colleagues, in future cases. Chief Justice Charles Evans Hughes stated that "[a] dissent in a court of last resort is an appeal to the brooding spirit of the law, to the intelligence of a future day, when a later decision may possibly correct the error into which the dissenting judge believes the court to have been betrayed" (Hughes 1928, 67–68). Dissenting opinions preserve the dialogue of previous Courts concerning questions of law, carrying those judicial conversations through time (Stack 1996). Dissents "connect the dialogue of generations of justices . . . with one another. These opinions enable the justices . . . to participate in an intertemporal conversation that may be a defining feature of the judiciary" (Stack 1996, 2257). The dissenting justices may thus pitch their dissent toward the future, with the hopes that, much like Justice Harlan's famous dissent in *Plessy v. Ferguson* (1896), their words will at some point be adopted and heralded by a future Court, even many decades into the future. For example, in *Pembaur v. City of Cincinnati*

(1986), Justice Powell directed his clerk to draft a dissent in order to "simply lay the foundation for what I hope will be an overruling of this unfortunate decision."[7] Similarly, in *Dow Chemical Co. v. United States* (1986), Justice Powell wrote his clerk: "I have every confidence that our dissents will be adopted by this Court in a future case."[8]

Sometimes this ultimate victory comes relatively quickly, and a justice who pens a dissent may still be on the Court to see that dissent become law. For example, Chief Justice Stone saw his dissents in *Tyson & Brother v. Banton* (1927) and *Ribnik v. McBride* (1928) become law in the state milk-regulation case *Nebbia v. New York* (1934) (see Mason 1956, 365–67). His dissents in *Minersville School District v. Gobitis* (1940) and *Jones v. City of Opelika* (1942) were similarly adopted by the majority in *West Virginia State Board of Education v. Barnette* (1943) when the Court struck down mandatory flag salute and pledge of allegiance laws for public schools. Former law clerk Sterling Carr wrote Chief Justice Stone in 1941, "Probably no man in the history of the Court has lived to see so many of his dissenting opinions become the law of the Court" (quoted in Mason 1956, 550). In fact, Alpheus Thomas Mason (1956, 550) reports that of the thirty-two precedents the Roosevelt Court later overturned, Chief Justice Stone had participated in thirteen of these decisions and dissented in ten, while Justice Brandeis took part in twenty cases and dissented in seventeen.

Second, a justice may write a dissent in the hopes of influencing those outside the courts. As Walter F. Murphy explained, "Publication of a dissent . . . is basically an attempt to shift the arena of combat. . . . Whether the author intends it or not, a dissent can become an appeal to contemporaries—to members of Congress, to the President, and executive officials, to lower court judges, to the bar or other interest groups, or to the public at large—to change the decision of the majority" (1964, 60).

Here, we identify two distinct groups justices may target: actors in other branches of government and the broader public. The legal and policy debate not only involves the courts, but also includes multiple actors and entities outside the courts. The process of bringing a court case can be viewed as formally inviting the courts to join in the legal and policy discussion; the courts' decisions are their contributions to this dialogue. These decisions are then read by members of the legislative and executive branches, outside interest groups, lawyers, potential future litigants, and the public.

Members of the legislative and executive branches write and implement the statutes courts are asked to interpret and may decide to amend these statutes in response to court decisions. This interbranch dialogue also guides members of the legislative and executive branches as they consider potential legislation. Justices' dissents may be written with the goal of influencing this future legislation. Justices may seek through their dissents to implore legislators to amend a badly written law or to enact entirely new legislation. Justice Ginsburg explained her dissent in *Ledbetter v. Goodyear Tire & Rubber Co.* (2007) as a "fit example" of a dissent that "aim[ed] to attract immediate public attention and, thereby, to propel legislative change" (Ginsburg 2010, 6). The dissent itself made clear its audience was not her fellow colleagues or lower court judges, but Congress, ending with this plea: "the ball is in Congress' court. As in 1991, the Legislature may act to correct this Court's parsimonious reading of Title VII." And Congress listened. Bills were introduced to amend Title VII with respect to when paycheck discrimination lawsuits could be filed within days of the Court's decision, and the Lilly Ledbetter Fair Pay Act became the first bill signed by President Barack Obama after his inauguration (Stolberg 2009).

Justices may similarly recognize that the current legal battle has been lost, but that the larger war may still be won. Vanessa A. Baird and Tonja Jacobi (2009) document how justices can use dissents to aid future litigants in reframing legal issues to be more palatable to a future Court. They specifically highlight when justices use their dissents to encourage litigants to pursue federalism-based arguments in order to achieve success. Another mechanism is spurring public/social mobilization that may then lead to change through avenues other than the courts. For example, Adam Sowards (2009) argues that Justice William O. Douglas's dissent in *Sierra Club v. Morton* (1972) played a strong role in helping to mobilize the broader public to join the American environmental movement.

The above discussion of motivations and goals for issuing dissents leads necessarily to a crucial question, and the central focus of this book: What motivates the majority to include a dissent in the ongoing dialogue? We argue that current majority opinion writers are more likely to feel a need to respond to those dissents that the majority believes pose a potential threat to the majority's position, while future majorities are more likely to include dissents that aid the majority. Specifically, we propose that majorities will include in the legal and policy dialogue those dissents that are well written and highly persuasive as well as those that are "attention-grabbing," that is, dissents that are more likely to attract external attention. We explicate this theory more fully below.

Short-Term Impact: To Respond or Not, That Is the Question

In any conversation, each participant must decide whether and how to respond to something said by the other. Sometimes, a detailed response is needed. Other times, a simple acknowledgment is all that is necessary. And, at times, the best response is no response at all. The same is true with respect to the justices on the Supreme Court. A dissent is a public statement of disagreement and dissension on the bench. But not all disagreements are equivalent, nor are all dissents equal. Rather, some dissents necessitate responses while others do not.

Once a dissent is drafted, the onus shifts to the majority opinion writer and the larger majority coalition to decide whether to respond. We ask specifically, when does the majority decide that it must respond to its dissenting colleagues in the majority opinion and counter their arguments? While previous studies explore why justices decide to dissent in particular cases (see, e.g., Ulmer 1970; Peterson 1981; Johnson, Black, and Ringsmuth 2008; Epstein, Landes, and Posner 2011), or investigate the potential external influences on and effects of the Court's dissents (see, e.g., Zink, Spriggs, and Scott 2009; Salamone 2014), we expand the current understanding of the role of dissents by providing a theory of why and when the majority is most likely to respond to a dissent by including the dissent in its final opinion.

We propose that the majority must make a strategic calculation about whether the best course of action is to respond to the dissent, or to ignore it. When the potential threat from a dissent increases, the majority will be more likely to decide it must address the dissent head on. If the majority deems the dissent to pose little to no threat to its position, however, then the majority can safely ignore it. We argue that how the dissent is written can influence the likelihood that the majority deems it a potential threat that must be answered. In particular, we highlight the potential influence of strong writing, as well as writing that increases the probability of the dissent's drawing external attention. We also identify additional factors about the dissent coalition that may similarly attract increased external notice, putting further pressure on the majority to respond.

First and foremost, a better-written dissent is more likely to draw a response from the majority than one that is not. No matter whether they are in the majority or the dissent, "justices wish to write legally strong, persuasive opinions" (Corley, Collins, and Calvin 2011, 34). Numerous scholars have examined how judges and justices strategically craft opinions in anticipation of responses by external actors. On the one hand, high-quality opinions help induce lower court (Corley and Wedeking 2014) and bureaucratic (Spriggs 1996) compliance. Language used in a Court's opinion has been linked to compliance and the strength of the Court's decision (Black et al. 2016, 2). On the other hand, Joshua Boston (2020) finds that federal circuit judges will strategically draft overly complex decisions in order to evade Supreme Court review while Ryan J. Owens, Justin Wedeking, and Patrick C. Wohlfarth (2013) suggest Supreme Court justices engage in similar behavior to evade congressional backlash.

We extend this reasoning to the behavior of the justices themselves. While the justices exchange ideas during oral arguments and in Conference, the primary outlet for the justices' internal dialogue comes in the exchange of written opinions. As Justice Anthony Kennedy stated, "[T]he purpose of the opinion is to convince . . . based on what we write" (Garner 2010, 85). Well-written opinions signal not only that care was taken in determining how best to express an argument, but also that care was likely taken in crafting the argument's substantive underpinnings as well. Justice Samuel Alito has argued that "there is a clear relationship between good, clear writing and good, clear thinking. And if you don't have one, it's very hard to have the other" (Garner 2010, 170). We therefore expect that more readable and clear opinions will be those that the majority will feel more pressured to respond to. Why? Because a readable, clear opinion is one that everyone—other justices, lower court judges, executive and legislative branch actors, members of the media, and the broader public—can understand. Such a dissent is not only more persuasive, but also more likely to receive more attention outside the Court, thus necessitating a response inside the Court. As Justice Scalia remarked: "When you write well, you capture the attention of your audience much better than when you write poorly" (Garner 2010, 53).

Based on our theorizing above, we further emphasize the use of analytic reasoning and precedent citation as factors that will push the majority to feel it necessary to respond to the dissent. A well-written opinion of this type will be one that will appeal to the justices, and also one that they may perceive as more likely to be viewed as a legitimate alternative by those outside the Court, and thus deserving of response. First, good legal writing reflects analytical thinking. Legal training includes learning to reason analytically (see, e.g., Russell 2000, 13). Skilled attorneys and judges must then ensure they transfer these analytical thinking skills into their written briefs and opinions. As Michael R. Smith (2008) aptly explains, "When a document contains strong legal analysis, it persuades first and most obviously through the substantive analysis itself, persuading readers through logic and reason, or logos. In addition to its logos function, however, strong analytical substance also persuades through ethos by selling the writer along with the writer's position. Legal writers who evince strong analytical skills through their writing are more effective in their efforts to persuade because the strong substance indicates to readers that they are intelligent and credible sources of information" (163).

Second, persuasive citation of precedent is an important component of strong legal writing. Precedent, or *stare decisis,* is the foundation of the American legal system. Courts rely on previous decisions answering similar questions, or precedent, for guidance in deciding cases. Although there is debate on the effect of prior decisions on Supreme Court decision-making (see, e.g., Brenner and Spaeth 1995; Spaeth and Segal 1999; Hansford and Spriggs 2006), it is expected that Supreme Court decisions will cite precedent. In fact, although Supreme Court justices rely on other legal and extralegal resources, "*stare decisis* predominates" (Epstein and Knight 1998, 172). Precedent operates by laying down the rules that subsequent courts apply to the case before them. The reasoning for the result is arguably the most important part of a legal opinion, and the "norm" is that legal reasoning relies on precedent to bolster the claims being made (Epstein and Knight 1998). Legal writing experts advise specifically that judges must ensure that their decisions are "'supported by adequate authority'" (Lebovits, Curtin, and Solomon 2008, 285). Thus, dissenting opinions that are analytical and well grounded in precedent are more likely to be perceived as stronger, well-reasoned, and persuasive. We argue that such opinions are more likely to compel the majority to respond.

Somewhat oppositely, a dissenting opinion that is highly disagreeable or angry may also be one that is more likely to prompt a response from the majority. Such an opinion draws a response not necessarily due to its persuasiveness, but rather due to its norm-bending nature. Over-the-top, angry dissenting language suggests the majority has not just simply erred, but issued a decision that has far-reaching, and potentially horrifying consequences. As Justice Scalia argued, "My tone is sometimes sharp. But I think sharpness is sometimes needed to demonstrate how much of a departure I believe the [majority decision] is" (Senior 2013). Michael Zilis and Justin Wedeking (2020) argue and find that justices will utilize disagreeable rhetoric when the issue is highly salient to them, even if the use of such language runs the risk of undermining collegial bargaining. A negative/angry opinion may also draw public and/or media attention, and even be written expressly for that purpose (see, e.g., Bryan and Ringsmuth 2016), increasing pressure on the majority to acknowledge the dissent's arguments in the majority opinion. Murphy (1964) further suggests members of Congress may be peculiarly "vulnerable to emotional appeals, especially when they suspect those same appeals may be arousing their constituents" (125). Majorities thus may feel pressured to respond in an attempt to mitigate the reach and impact of dissents that appear designed to engage with external actors.

Similarly, certain writing styles may make a dissent stand out and attract external attention. Writing guides caution against the overuse of adverbs and adjectives, if not advocating eliminating certain words entirely (see, e.g., Garner 2002; Enquist and Oates 2009;). One writing expert explained: "Because generations of writers have overused words like 'clearly' and 'very,' these and other common intensifiers have become virtually meaningless. As a matter of fact, they have begun to develop a connotation exactly opposite their original meaning. So many writers (lawyers and judges alike) have used those labels in place of well-reasoned analysis that some readers see these intensifiers as signaling a weak analysis" (Edwards 2010, 229).

We suggest, however, that the use of intensifiers play a different role in terms of spurring a majority to react to a dissenting opinion. Their usage makes writing more lively and thus more likely to be noticed. We build here on Lance N. Long and William H. Christensen's (2013) theory of argumentative threat: "The idea is that those who agree with us are generally good, and therefore we use general terms indicating that their good acts pervade the entire group and are the norm. Conversely, a bad act is described with specificity so as to limit its application to the specific situation" (947). The authors examine US Supreme Court dissenting opinions, finding that dissenting opinions contain more intensifiers than majority opinions, suggesting the use of intensifiers increases as a response to perceived threat. They conclude that "this increased use of intensifiers could be a form of linguistic intergroup bias in the sense that a dissenting judge, alienated from the majority, seeks to show that the dissenting argument is 'obviously,' 'clearly,' and 'wholly' superior to the opinion of what is now the dissenter's out-group. The increased use of intensifiers . . . could be a subconscious attempt at showing the 'strength' of the dissenter's argument — even though the dissenter consciously knows that using more intensifiers is negatively perceived by judges and legal readers in general" (948). Although such argumentative threats may be viewed as "bad" writing, they also may increase the potential threat the dissent poses to the majority. A dissent that utilizes a high percentage of intensifying language is both trying to show the strength of the dissenting opinion while also signaling that the majority opinion is a clear threat to the law and perhaps American society. The strong identification of such threats in a dissent may therefore push the majority to directly address the dissent to try to neutralize potential external backlash.

We include distinctive or memorable language as an additional writing tool that may spur external attention, and thus create more of a threat for the majority. The argument with respect to distinctive language is similar to that of intensifiers—dissenting language that draws attention from the reader, and stands apart from the norm, offers a greater level of rhetorical threat to the majority opinion than writing that is calm, measured, and uses routine language. Much like negative emotional language, studies find that people are more likely to remember writings and phrases that use distinctive words (see, e.g., Danescu-Niculsecu-Mizil et al. 2012; Coscia 2014). And, at least anecdotally, the use of distinctive phrases in dissents raises the likelihood of media attention; for example, Rachael K. Hinkle and Michael J. Nelson (2018) point to the widespread coverage of Justice Scalia's dissent in *King v. Burwell* (2015) (after calling the majority opinion "pure applesauce") and Justice Ginsburg's dissent in *Shelby County v. Holder* (2013) (likening the Court's decision to "throwing away your umbrella in a rainstorm because you are not getting wet"). Hinkle and Nelson find that an increased use of distinctive language and negative emotional words leads to an increased likelihood of a dissent being cited by a future Supreme Court majority. We extend their reasoning to argue that such memorable language has a short-term impact as well, forcing the current Court majority to try to blunt the impact of these attention-grabbing dissents through a discussion of the dissent in the majority opinion.

Next, we propose that certain facets of the dissenting coalition may increase the likelihood of a dissent attracting significant external attention, in turn increasing the likelihood the majority will feel forced to respond. One, the majority likely feels most threatened, and thus most likely to go on the defensive, when the dissenting coalition is larger. Dissents highlight dissension, but dissension by many is more powerful than dissension by one. A dissent by a single justice can be written off as an idiosyncratic response while a four-justice dissent wields much more weight.

Two, we argue that external actors will pay attention to who is dissenting. Is the dissent simply another liberal-conservative split? Or does the dissent reflect an ideologically heterogeneous coalition of dissenters? The latter grouping is much more likely to draw external notice, as it suggests the disagreement reflected in the dissent is more than a simple ideological difference of opinion. Previous studies of legislative signaling (see, e.g., Gilligan and Krehbiel 1989; Kessler and Krehbiel 1996) as well as amicus brief signaling (see, e.g., Goelzhauser and Vouvalis 2015) find that external actors perceive heterogeneous coalitions as producing higher-quality products and transmitting more credible signals and information. Similarly, a heterogeneous dissent coalition signals to other actors and the public that theirs is a position worthy of attention, and one also worthy of response by the majority. Majority opinion writers will feel more pressure to cite a dissent when the dissent cannot be easily written off as a simple ideological squabble. Instead, dissents that reflect the old adage "politics makes for strange bedfellows" will pose more of a threat to the strength and credibility of the majority opinion, prompting a response.

Three, relationships on the Court matter, and so the identity of the dissenting justice(s), particularly in relation to the identity of the majority opinion author, likely matters when the majority decides whether to respond. Here, we focus on the ideological distance between the majority median and the dissenting coalition median. We argue that a majority that is relatively close to the dissent in terms of overall ideology will feel more of a need to address the arguments raised by the dissenter(s) than when they are ideologically distant.

Continuing the Dialogue: Citing the Dissent in the Future

For future Court majorities, the calculations of the majority change somewhat. In order for a future majority to cite a past dissent positively, first it must be remembered. The dissent must also be perceived as persuasive and helpful to the arguments made by the majority. Thus, we propose that future majorities will again be more likely to cite a past dissent when the dissent is better written and more well reasoned (more readable, analytical, and citing more precedent), and when the dissent uses more adverbs and adjectives (including intensifiers), uncommon language (see Hinkle and Nelson 2018), and highly negative emotional language. Previous studies find that people are much more apt to remember information that stimulates negative emotions as compared to information that elicits positive emotions (see, e.g., D'Argembeau and Van der Linden 2005). In sum, we argue that dissents that initially captured the attention of the majority are also more likely to be memorable and thus more likely to be cited by future majorities seeking support for their arguments.

We further argue that future majorities are more likely to cite a past dissent when the dissent coalition is larger. Majority opinion writers are well aware that decisions with dissents are more likely to be overruled by a future Court (Ulmer 1970; Brenner, Spaeth, and Hagle 1990; Canon and Johnson 1999; Spriggs and Hansford 2001; Way and Turner 2006; Corley 2010). Thus, when the dissenting coalition is larger, its reach into the future is likely to be more powerful than a dissent written by a solo justice.

For future Court majorities, there is also the question of how enmeshed in the dialogue the dissent is. According to Thomas G. Hansford and James F. Spriggs II (2006), Supreme Court justices respond to the vitality of precedent. Precedents that have been positively interpreted over time are more authoritative and possess greater legal weight, whereas precedents that have been negatively treated over time have diminished legal authority. We extend their theory of precedent vitality to dissents. We argue that if a dissent is positively cited by majority opinions over time, that dissent becomes increasingly part of the continuing dialogue and therefore more likely to be positively cited in the future.

Finally, we expect that if a dissent was cited by the contemporary majority in the same case, future majorities are more likely to cite that dissent because it is already part of the legal and policy conversation. However, if the majority opinion that accompanied the dissent has been overruled, there is less need for a future majority opinion to cite the dissent. Instead, the majority opinion will cite the overruling majority opinion. For example, after *Bowers v. Hardwick* (1986) was overruled by *Lawrence v. Texas* (2003), there was no need to cite Justice Stevens's dissent in *Bowers*; instead, majority opinions could cite *Lawrence*. Thus, we do not expect future majority opinions to cite dissents that accompanied a majority opinion that has been subsequently overruled.

Overall, we present a novel theory explaining the potential effect of dissents, and how dissents do—and do not—become part of the larger legal and policy dialogue. We propose that when a dissent is issued, the majority coalition must determine whether to respond directly to the dissent or to ignore it. The majority's goal is to present the strongest possible decision of the Court to the country. While a dissent by definition suggests disagreement, not all dissents are created equal, nor do all dissents pose a threat to the strength of the majority opinion. Additionally, not all dissents will help a future majority opinion. We argue that the contemporaneous majority will ignore dissents unless the majority determines that the dissent poses a particular threat. For dissents that pose a threat, the majority will discuss them in the majority opinion, thus enmeshing these dissents in the broader legal and policy dialogue. Alternatively, we argue that future majority opinions will ignore dissents unless the majority remembers the dissent and then determines that the dissent will aid the current majority. What do these threatening and/or memorable dissents look like? We propose that they are readable, well grounded in precedent, and highly analytic, as well as more likely to draw external attention from other political actors, the media, or the public. We argue that dissents that display these characteristics are ultimately more likely to be included in the current and future legal and policy debate. We test this theory in chapters 4 and 5 of the book.

Outline of the Book

To fully explore why certain dissents become part of the intra-Court dialogue while others do not, chapter 1 begins by tracing the development of certain institutional norms and practices on the Court that, combined, have worked to move the Court from a norm of acquiescence to a culture of dissent. This historical assessment focuses specifically on structural changes—such as the elimination of the Court's discretionary docket, the addition of the syllabus, and the formalization of dissent assignment procedures, among others—that help to enable, if not encourage, dissenting behavior. We then systematically assess when and why justices are more or less likely to dissent from the majority in the modern era. The results of this chapter mirror those of past studies, highlighting the importance of ideological and strategic considerations on justices' voting decisions. Our results also reveal support for an additional, notable explanation for dissenting behavior: the role of legal certainty. When external signals suggest the level of legal certainty is high and a single legal answer predominates, justices are less likely to dissent. Comparatively, when the level of legal certainty is low and confusion over the "correct" legal answer abounds, so too does dissensus on the high court. These results underline the importance of accounting for the role law can play in constraining justices' ability to freely express their policy positions in all cases.

Chapter 2 then turns to the question of what happens when justices begin thinking about crafting a dissent and hoping to find support among their colleagues. We provide one of the first-ever accounts of the dissent coalition-formation process. We investigate the dissent coalition-formation process in order to understand the bargaining and accommodation that occurs to shape the content of the dissent. Through an assessment of the archived papers of

Justices Lewis Powell and Harry Blackmun, we explore what dissent coalition negotiation and bargaining comprises. We discover that dissenters work hard to try to sway majority members to join them and, failing that, to craft a strong dissent that reflects the consensus of the dissenting coalition. Much like with the majority, bargaining can be intense, with dissenters trying to stave off additional separate opinions or a weakening of the dissenting coalition. We argue that understanding this process of dissent coalition formation, bargaining, and negotiation aids us in understanding why some dissents become a part of the larger legal and policy debate while others do not.

Chapters 3 and 4 then address the central question of this book: What leads a dissent to become part of the broader legal and policy dialogue? Chapter 3 examines the contemporaneous impact of Supreme Court dissents—namely the effect of a dissenting opinion on the majority opinion in the same case. In other words, when does the majority respond to the dissent by citing it in the majority opinion? Chapter 4 then addresses when future Supreme Court majority opinions positively cite previous dissents. Taken together, these two chapters offer strong support for our theory of argumentative threat and re-action: majorities are more likely to cite dissents both now and in the future when they are well written and when they are more likely to draw external attention. Importantly, we also find that what that looks like differs in important ways for contemporaneous as opposed to future Courts. Contemporaneous courts are most likely to respond to dissents that use high levels of analytical thinking and are well grounded in precedent, as well as those that use a high number of adverbs, adjectives, and intensifiers. Future courts are alternatively most likely to positively cite prior dissents that are well grounded in precedent, but also those that use writing tools that increase future recall—those that utilize a more narrative style, a high degree of intensifiers, and a high degree of memorable language. In sum, we find that dissenting justices can strategically write their opinions in ways that increase the likelihood of provoking a response from the majority, as well as ensuring the dissent becomes a part of the legal and policy discourse. Finally, the conclusion summarizes our findings and explores their broader implications.

Contributions

This study makes a number of important contributions to the broader literature on Supreme Court decision-making and internal Court negotiations. First, we offer a novel and comprehensive theory for understanding why certain dissents become a part of the national legal and policy dialogue, both now and in the future, while others are consigned to the dusty pages of federal court reporters. While previous studies have aided us in understanding why justices may dissent, and also how dissents can influence the calculations of the majority coalition and the majority opinion author, we offer an assessment of how a published dissent may, or may not, influence the broader debate over law and policy in the United States. The majority's calculations of how to handle a dissent do not end once a set of justices decide definitively not to join the majority's opinion. Rather, the majority now must decide whether to continue the justices' debate publicly through its opinion or cut it off. Future majority opinion authors must similarly decide whether to include prior dissents in their opinions—in other words, whether or not those dissents will continue to be part of the overall conversation. Our theory helps explicate how the writing choices dissenting justices make may influence these crucial decisions.

Second, we take the important step of extending the notion of "dialogue" on the Court beyond just constitutional cases to encompass the whole of the Court's output. A narrow focus on the Court's constitutional dialogue—where perhaps the Court's role is most prominently on display—obscures the multitude of ways the Court, and the justices' ongoing communication, truly influences the broader legal and policy discussion. Dissents may actually have the biggest external impact in statutory cases where they may compel Congress to act or the public to get involved. Statutory cases do not as easily prompt titillating headlines, but they are, perhaps ironically, where the Court's and the justices' ongoing influence on policymaking is most clearly identifiable. We thus seek to understand the totality of the Court's impact in crafting national policy.

Third, while many prior studies examine dissensus at the aggregate level, relatively few look at dissensus at the individual level. Thus, we advance our understanding of the conditions that lead individual justices to dissent. Additionally, we offer the first systematic assessment of the potential constraining role of law on these decisions. Extending our prior work on unanimity (Corley, Steigerwalt, and Ward 2013), we investigate the degree to which legal certainty—the notion that one particular legal answer may be more "correct" than any other—influences the expression, and suppression, of dissent. Mirroring our earlier findings, we find that justices are less likely to dissent when the level of legal certainty is high, pushing the justices toward a single point of legal agreement. Dissents are more likely, alternatively, when the level of legal certainty is low and multiple opposing legal arguments exist. These findings illuminate the central role law plays even in the expression of disagreement among the justices.

Fourth, we also offer the first detailed assessment of dissent coalition formation, bargaining, and negotiations. Prior studies have included entreaties from dissenting justices into their assessments of majority coalition deliberations, but none to date have focused on the dissenters' internal discussions. We use the papers of Justices Powell and Blackmun to identify the nature of these negotiations, offering an original look at both the ways in which dissenters work to craft strong dissents and stave off additional separate opinions as well as the peculiarities of another facet of the justices' internal discussions. This book therefore sheds fresh light on how the dissenting coalition members interact with each other.

Fifth, our results speak to the importance of language in Supreme Court opinions. Legal scholars study the opinions of the Court, dissecting their language in an effort to understand the law. Practitioners analyze and study the content of Court opinions in order to provide legal advice to their clients, using cases to predict what courts will do in a specific case that has yet to come before them. It is the rationale used in the past that provides guidance for the future. The words used, the reasoning employed, and the tests devised by the Court are important to understand. Thus, court *opinions* matter, not just the vote on the merits, and understanding how the opinion-writing process works is central to explaining the development of the law. We reinforce the point that "explorations of the Supreme Court should not begin and end with examination of the vote . . . [but] must explore the range of choices that contribute to the development of the law" (Epstein and Knight 1998, 185). We extend this idea to encompass the choices made by the dissenting coalition. Dissents not only make their own, independent contributions to the broader legal and policy debate, but they also have the potential to shape the content of the majority opinion and thus the Court's contribution to the policy deliberations. Although previous studies have focused on the content of the majority opinion and concurring opinions, this study provides a comprehensive understanding of the content of dissenting opinions and the extent to which dissenting coalition members can alter opinion language to improve the probability that the dissent will become an important part of the conversation regarding law and policy. It is only by understanding the choices made by dissent authors, and how those choices in turn influence majority opinion authors, that we can fully understand the development of law overall.

Finally, this book illustrates the benefits of utilizing computerized text analysis to further our understanding of political behavior. Text analysis software enables us to examine the totality of decisions issued by the Court over an extended time period. By relying on a substantial quantity of textual data we are able to examine the language the justices employ during the dissenting opinion-writing process and, consequently, are better able to assess the role of language more broadly on the development of law. We turn now to chapter 1 to begin our examination of the practice and process of dissenting on the United States Supreme Court.

1 | Dissenting Behavior on the US Supreme Court

T HE US SUPREME COURT is currently entrenched in an era of dissensus. During the 2018 term of the Court, only 39 percent of cases were decided unanimously. The other 61 percent of cases had at least one dissenting vote, and 28 percent of the Court's decisions were decided 5–4. For the first almost 150 years of the Court, however, there were high levels of unanimity (see figure 1). It was not until 1943 that less than a majority of the Court's decisions were non-unanimous, and as recently as the 1940 term, 72 percent of the Court's cases were decided unanimously.

What happened to shift the Court from a norm of consensus to the modern era of dissensus? Why did a Court that prioritized speaking with a single voice shift over the centuries to become one where individual positions are prioritized? In order to fully understand dissents on the Supreme Court, we must first appreciate how dissensus became the norm. The first half of this chapter traces the rise of the modern era of dissensus from the creation of the Court until today, focusing on major formal and informal institutional changes on the Court that helped move it away from an era of consensus and acquiescence. Each of the structural changes we highlight enabled dissent to flourish.

The second half of this chapter then investigates what leads a justice in the modern era to dissent in a particular case. In the introduction, we highlighted a number of motivations for dissents: to put disagreement in the public record, to persuade future Courts or legislatures to change the law, and to spur change in other arenas, to name a few. Regardless of the goals justices have when writing their dissents, they must first make the decision to dissent. We propose a comprehensive model for understanding dissenting behavior that takes into account personal policy preferences, strategic considerations, the institutional context, and legal factors. Our theoretical framework is the first to take into account the potential effect legal constraints may have on the decision of whether or not a justice dissents. We then empirically test this theoretical model to discern why and when justices are most likely to decide to dissent in the modern era of dissensus.

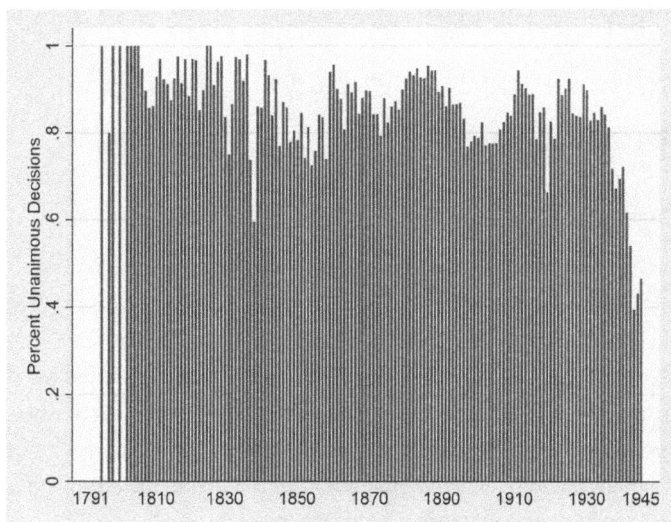

FIGURE 1. Percentage of unanimous decisions by Supreme Court term, 1791–1945

Jealousy Preserved Individualism: Dissenting Behavior in Historical Perspective

The first published dissent on the US Supreme Court appeared in the 1793 case *Georgia v. Brailsford*. Justice James Iredell wrote: "It is my misfortune to dissent from the opinion entertained by the rest of the court upon the present occasion; but I am bound to decide, according to the dictates of my own judgments" (416). Justice John Blair followed Justice Iredell's lead, writing: "My sentiments have coincided till this moment with the sentiments entertained by the majority of the court; but a doubt has just occurred, which I think it my duty to declare" (417–18). Chief Justice John Jay made no comment on the dissents other than that he was writing for "all the court, except the judges who have just delivered their sentiments" (418).

Even though the above dissent appeared relatively quickly after the Court's formation, the Court's earliest years were typified by extremely high levels of consensus. The justices issued most of their opinions institutionally, with a single opinion "By the Court" to resolve the case—what the Court today calls "per curiam." Of the sixty-three cases decided from 1790 to 1800, forty-five (71%) were decided this way (Kelsh 1999, 140). Ironically, these early years are instead best known for the English common-law practice of delivering "seriatim opinions" (a series of opinions), meaning that each justice issued an opinion, in ascending order of seniority, in each case (see, e.g., Rotunda 2017). In order to determine the position of each justice on the issues involved, each opinion had to be read in full. Did a majority agree on the outcome and reasoning? Who disagreed and why? Still, only fifteen of the sixty-three early cases (24%) were decided seriatim, making it somewhat of a misnomer to describe these early years as ones of seriatim or individual expression (Kelsh 1999).

When seriatim opinions were issued, however, it was due to division among the justices and the importance of the case, such as whether it was a constitutional decision likely to be covered by the press (ZoBell 1959; Currie 1985; Kelsh 1999). For example, in *Chisholm v. Georgia* (1793), Justice Iredell's opinion was published first, as he was the newest member of the Court. He explained that states could not be sued in federal court without their consent. The subsequent four opinions by Justices Blair, James Wilson, William Cushing, and Chief Justice Jay, however, took the opposite position, constituting a majority. Alarmed at the decision, and encouraged by Justice Iredell's "dissent," the states called for a constitutional amendment to overturn the decision. In 1795, the Eleventh Amendment was ratified, quickly making Justice Iredell's position the law of the land, and prompting Chief Justice Jay to resign for the more powerful and influential position of governor of New York.

In order to increase the Court's power and stature, Chief Justice Oliver Ellsworth attempted, and largely failed, to completely eradicate the practice of delivering seriatim opinions by instead adopting a single "Opinion of the Court" delivered unanimously and anonymously (Warren 1932; ZoBell 1959; Marcus 2007). For example, Chief Justice Ellsworth began his opinion in *Brown v. Barry* (1797): "In delivering the opinion of the court..." (367). While no other opinions were issued in that case, it was rare for the chief or any other justice to state that he was speaking on behalf of the rest of his colleagues.

Where Chief Justice Ellsworth failed, his successor, Chief Justice John Marshall, succeeded. In Chief Justice Marshall's first case, *Talbot v. Seeman* (1801), he authored and issued a single opinion speaking for the entire Court; importantly, the published opinion also noted Chief Justice Marshall's role as the author on behalf of the Court majority. He would routinely succeed in doing so during his more than three-decade tenure as chief. Justices other than the chief also issued unanimous Opinions of the Court under their own names, largely when Chief Justice Marshall was absent or otherwise not participating in the case. Yet, Chief Justice Marshall's habit of issuing an institutional opinion, often with no additional individual opinions by the other justices, did not go unnoticed. Thomas Jefferson, who regularly found himself on opposite sides from the chief justice, complained that "an opinion is huddled up in conclave, perhaps by a majority of one, delivered as if unanimous, and with the silent acquiescence of lazy or timid associates, by a crafty chief judge" (quoted in Jackson 1969, 24).

One direct, yet likely unintentional, outgrowth of justices now issuing opinions, including unanimous majority opinions, under their own names was a desire to ensure individual doctrinal, intellectual, and ideological consistency. If a justice believed his vote would contradict a position he had publicly taken in a previous case, he was more likely to issue a separate opinion reaffirming his historical position. For example, Justice Bushrod Washington wrote in dissent in *Mason v. Haile* (1827, 379): "A regard for my own consistency, and that, too, upon a great constitutional question, compels me to record the reasons upon which my dissent is founded." Over time, this concern for consistency morphed into concern for judicial reputation more broadly, further fueling the incentive to dissent.

Dissents increased under Chief Justice Roger Taney. Under Chief Justice Marshall, just 11 percent of the Court's decisions contained a dissent, whereas the Court increased its dissent rate to 20 percent during Chief Justice Taney's tenure (1836–64), caused at least in part by the 1838 increase in the number of justices from seven to nine. Doctrinal consistency was increasingly cited by the justices, in addition to constitutional and important issues, as the reasons for issuing dissents (Kelsh 1999). For example, Justice Joseph Story explained in *Briscoe v. Commonwealth Bank of Kentucky* (1837):

> I am of opinion (as I have already intimated) that upon constitutional questions, the public have a right to know the opinion of every judge who dissents from the opinion of the Court, and the reasons of his dissent. I have another and strong motive—my profound reverence and affection for the dead. Mr. Chief Justice Marshall is not here to speak for himself, and knowing full well the grounds of his opinion [in a prior case], in which I concurred, that this act is unconstitutional, I have felt an earnest desire to vindicate his memory from the imputation of rashness or want of deep reflection. Had he been living, he would have spoken in the joint names of both of us. (350)

Justice Peter V. Daniel, also known as one of the "great dissenters," took this desire for consistency to another level: the perpetual dissent, akin to "an act of civil disobedience" (Larsen 2008, 476). After issuing an initial dissent on a particular legal question, Justice Daniel would continue to issue dissents in subsequent cases on the same issue, reiterating his initial position. For example, in *The Propeller Monticello v. Mollison* (1854), Justice Daniel wrote in dissent: "My purpose is simply to maintain my own consistency in adhering to convictions which are in nowise weakened" (156). Harold J. Spaeth and Jeffrey A. Segal (1999) determined that "Daniel is perhaps the most unyielding among the Taney Court justices in sustaining his preferences" (67). Justice Daniel went so far as to issue seventeen different dissents in his seventeen years on the Court over a single issue: the question of federal jurisdiction over corporate lawsuits (Kelman 1985).

Justices also increasingly noted their dissenting votes, even when they declined to write a full dissenting opinion (Fife et al. 2017). The notation was often followed by a brief rationale. For example, in *Winans v. New York & Erie Railroad Co.* (1858): "Mr. Justice DANIEL dissents, on the ground of a want of jurisdiction" (103). Noting a concurrence or dissent was rare under Chief Justice Marshall, occurring only 41 times. By contrast, the Taney Court did so a whopping 389 times (Blaustein and Mersky 1978, 137–41). Madelyn Fife and colleagues (2017) tie the increased use of notation in this period to those more "mundane" cases comprising the Court's mandatory docket.

For most of the Taney Court, justices' dissents were exceedingly respectful and even apologetic toward the majority. Dissenters wrote that they regretted expressing disagreement with their colleagues, whom they said they respected greatly. For example, Justice William Johnson's first Supreme Court dissent in *Ex parte Bollman* (1807) began: "In this case I have the misfortune to dissent from the majority of my brethren. As it is a case of much interest, I feel it incumbent upon me to assign the reasons upon which I [dissent]." (101).

Toward the end of Chief Justice Taney's tenure, however, the tone of some dissents began to change. Instead of respect and regret, dissenters now attacked the majority with negative, sometimes harsh, language. In *Fontain v. Ravenel* (1854), Justice Daniel wrote in dissent: "In expressing my dissent, I shall not follow the protracted argument [of the majority] throughout its entire length; my purpose is, chiefly, to free myself on any future occasion from the trammels of an assent, either expressed or implied, to what are deemed by me the untenable, and, in this case, the irrelevant positions which . . . [the majority's] argument propounds" (396).

In the post–Civil War era, one of the apologetic rationales for expressing dissent—public interest and importance—was abandoned by the justices. They instead added new, more specific justifications, such as a belief that

the majority was departing from precedent, or that the consequences of the
Court's decision would be far-reaching, grave, injurious, serious, or alarming
(Kelsh 1999). For example, Justice Mahlon Pitney explained in his dissent
in *Southern Pacific Co. v. Jensen* (1917): "I deem it proper, in view of the mo-
mentous consequences of the decision, to present some additional considerations" (223). Another justification for dissent, one that began under Taney
but became more common during this period, was simple disagreement. Justice Samuel Freeman Miller wrote in *Sykes v. Chadwick* (1873): "I regret to
have to dissent, but I think the precedent of making laws in this manner too
pernicious to be acquiesced in by my silence" (151).

While the overall dissent rate remained low, especially compared to modern times, the justices increasingly viewed the Court less as an institution and
more as a collection of individuals, with each justice progressively concerned
about consistency and maintaining his reputation. Chief Justice Salmon P.
Chase took three pages of his dissent in the *Legal Tender Cases* (1871, 575–
77) to explain how his judicial position was consistent with the position he
had espoused as secretary of the treasury. As justices became more concerned
about maintaining consistency in their own judicial records, their colleagues
also began noting their apparent inconsistencies. For example, Justice Oliver Wendell Holmes Jr. wrote in *Smoot Sand & Gravel Corp. v. Washington
Airport, Inc.* (1931) that "it is to be noticed that Mr. Justice Day who wrote
the earlier decision took part also in the latter and seems to have agreed with
it" (350). Dissents were also now increasingly cited in subsequent cases. In
Myers v. United States (1926), Justice James McReynolds wrote in dissent: "In
an elaborate dissent Mr. Justice Field, Mr. Justice Gray and Mr. Justice Brown
expressed the view that it was beyond the President's power to remove the
judge of any court during the term for which appointed. They necessarily re-
pudiated the doctrine of illimitable power" (225).

Perhaps the most important development of the post–Civil War era was
the increased pace of Supreme Court precedents overturned by subsequent
cases, with dissents from the original cases used as support for invalidating
the precedent. For example, Justice Samuel Freeman Miller's dissent in *Hepburn v. Griswold* (1870), which was joined by Justices Noah Swayne and David Davis, was cited and discussed at multiple points in the overruling *Legal
Tender Cases* (1871). Justice McReynolds's dissent in *Myers* was similarly the
blueprint for the majority opinion in *Humphrey's Executor v. United States*
(1935). Dissents can also be vindicated when precedent is overturned by constitutional amendment, as was the case for Justice Benjamin Curtis's dissent

in *Dred Scott v. Sandford* (1857) with the passage of the Thirteenth and Fourteenth Amendments. These developments bolstered the growing notion that
the Court was a collection of individual jurists with their own views of the law
rather than a cohesive institution acting collectively.

While chief justices of the era such as William Taft attempted to minimize
dissension, Chief Justice Taft himself may have unwittingly engineered a key
institutional change that led to greater dissensus. He established a committee
of justices, led by Willis Van Devanter, to draft a bill to give the Court greater
control over its docket; the Judge's Bill of 1925 was subsequently successfully
enacted. It greatly reduced the number of mandatory cases the justices were
required to decide and allowed them greater freedom to make their own se-
lections. It was not long before the Court's docket became filled with the most
contentious issues of the day, leading to greater opportunities for the justices
to disagree. Dissent rates climbed as a result (Halpern and Vines 1977).

This period on the Court also saw the growth of more discernible dissenting coalition blocs, exemplified by the duo of Justices Holmes and Louis
Brandeis. A 1927 *St. Louis Post-Dispatch* article explained, "Oliver Wendell
Holmes and Louis Dembitz Brandeis have achieved a spiritual kinship that
marks them off as a separate liberal chamber of the Supreme Court . . . these
two are nearly always together; often they are together against the rest of the
court" (quoted in Faulkner 1958, 176). Justices joining the Court after Justices Holmes and Brandeis were even less likely to acquiesce to the majority
than their predecessors (Pritchett 1948). By the end of this era, C. Herman
Pritchett's 1941 analysis of the 1939–41 terms of the Court reveals two distinct, cohesive dissenting blocks, with Chief Justice Charles Evan Hughes,
Justices McReynolds, Owen J. Roberts, and Harlan Fiske Stone comprising
one group, and Justices Frank W. Murphy, Felix Frankfurter, Hugo L. Black,
and William O. Douglas encompassing the other. Most notably, in only two
out of eighty-nine total dissents did a dissenting coalition reflect any type of
allegiances across these blocs (Pritchett 1941, 892–93). Toward the end of his
tenure, Chief Justice Hughes recognized this transformation. When Justice
Douglas joined the Court in 1939, Chief Justice Hughes told him: "I think
you will find after you have been on the bench for a while that in a great majority of the cases, perhaps in two-thirds of them, the judges will ultimately
reach agreement and announce opinions that are unanimous. But in at least
a third of the cases, agreement will not be possible. In those cases there will
be dissents—no matter how carefully the judges were chosen—whether one
President or several Presidents selected them" (Douglas 1948, 104).[1] Marcus E.

Hendershot and colleagues (2013) find empirical evidence of the fracturing coalition under Chief Justice Hughes, which was obscured through previous studies that used opinion-based measures of dissent.

By 1941, when Justice Stone was elevated to chief justice, a culture of dissent was entrenched on the Court. The new age of dissent had less to do with justices simply disagreeing more often and more to do with their willingness to express that dissent outside of the Conference (Walker, Epstein, and Dixon 1988; Caldeira and Zorn 1998; Post 2001). For example, Lee Epstein, Jeffrey A. Segal, and Harold J. Spaeth (2001) find that while the Court under Chief Justice Morrison Waite (1874–88) publicly exhibited dissenting votes in 9 percent of its decisions, the justices actually disagreed in their private Conference 40 percent of the time. Comparatively, under Chief Justice Stone, 45 percent of cases contained dissents (Epstein, Segal, and Spaeth 2001). The transformation from the private acquiescence exhibited under Chief Justice Waite to increasing public dissent was the result of broader societal developments that made adherence to precedent untenable (Bennett et al. 2018). Progressive economic and social legislation passed from the end of the nineteenth century to the mid-twentieth century faced vehement opposition from conservatives who found a sympathetic institution in the Supreme Court. Progressive justices fought back, publicly airing their disagreements. Once progressives held the majority, their dissents became law, and conservatives dissented to reiterate their formerly majority positions. Legal realism, the notion that judges were results-oriented and employed post hoc rationales for their personal preferences, was pervasive during this period (see, e.g., Pound 1922; Llewellyn 1934).

With a discretionary docket of contentious cases and the value of precedent in dispute, the norm of dissensus took hold. An academic atmosphere also flourished as former law professors treated judicial opinions as if they were law review articles. Justices like John Marshall Harlan II (16.5%), John Paul Stevens (16.2%), and Douglas (14.5%) issued dissents in nearly one out of every five cases. And the Court as a whole embraced this new culture: between the 1939 and 1942 terms, the proportion of cases with a dissent jumped from 15 percent to 54 percent (Walker, Epstein, and Dixon 1988).

Departing from previous chief justices, Chief Justice Stone strenuously defended dissents. In 1942, Chief Justice Stone gave an address to a judicial conference and subsequently published it in a law journal under the title: "Dissenting Opinions Are Not without Value." He explained that dissents are most valuable as "intellectual" statements that appeal to "scholarship, history and reason" for "shaping and sometimes in altering the course of law" (Stone 1942, 78).

Chief Justice Stone also aided the entrenchment of dissents as normal practice by leading the way in creating a norm of bargaining and accommodation during the opinion-writing process. Before multiple opinions were issued, the justices wrestled with the counterarguments of their colleagues, and opinions could be improved. When in dissent, Chief Justice Stone provided leadership by negotiating with the other dissenters, as well as the members of the majority, so that all the opinions—both majority and dissenting—would be strengthened (Mason 1956). His innovation was so effective that it continues to this day. Negotiating and bargaining both within and between majority and minority coalitions became institutionalized.

As the number of dissents exploded under Chief Justice Stone, another new practice was also quickly established: concurring opinions written solely to respond to the dissent. This development further bolstered the legitimacy and importance of dissents. For example, in *Federal Power Commissioner v. Hope Natural Gas Co.* (1944), Justices Black and Murphy wrote: "We agree with the Court's opinion and would add nothing to what has been said but for what is patently a wholly gratuitous assertion as to Constitutional law in the dissent of Mr. Justice Frankfurter" (619).

Given the longstanding concern for individual consistency, justices also began issuing concurrences to explain why they were *not* dissenting in cases where they might be expected to because of their prior positions on issues. Justice Robert Jackson issued this concurrence after reading Justice Black's dissent in *Magnolia Petroleum Co. v. Hunt* (1943): "I concur with the opinion of the Chief Justice. If the Court were to reconsider *Williams v. North Carolina*, 317 U.S. 287, in the light of the views expressed by Mr. Justice Black, I should adhere to the views I expressed in dissent there. Until we do so, I consider myself bound by that decision" (447).

Fred Vinson took over as chief justice in 1946. By the time Vinson joined the Court, the Court had transitioned from a self-conscious and apologetic posture toward dissents to one of unabashed pride. Before the start of the 1948 term, Justice Douglas gave a speech to the American Bar Association that was subsequently published in a law journal with the title "Dissent: A Safeguard of Democracy." Justice Douglas defended dissent as inherent in a democracy: "Disagreement among judges is as true to the character of democracy as freedom of speech itself. The dissenting opinion is as genuinely American as Otis' denunciation of the general warrants, as Thomas Paine's, Thomas Jefferson's, or James Madison's briefs for civil liberties" (1948, 105). He further stressed that dissent during times of crisis can have important future effects: "[Judges'] dissents or concurring opinions may salvage for tomorrow the principle that was sacrificed or forgotten today. Their discussion and propagation of the great principles of our Charter may keep the democratic ideal alive in days of regression, uncertainty, and despair" (107).

The next year, before the start of the 1949 term, Chief Justice Vinson addressed the same group. He echoed many of Justice Douglas's remarks and took considerable time explaining the importance of dissents. Citing the 1925 Judge's Bill, he argued that "the very nature of the Supreme Court's jurisdiction is such that the easy cases, the clear and indisputable cases, very seldom come before the Court. Our discretionary certiorari jurisdiction encompasses, for the most part, only the borderline cases—those in which there is conflict among lower courts or widespread uncertainty regarding problems of national importance" (1949, 1273). And, by 1961, justices believed separate opinions needed no defense. In a 1961 memorandum to the other justices at the start of Justice Frankfurter's final term on the Court, Justice Douglas demonstrated how far the Court had moved away from the previous norm of acquiescence: "I defend the right of any justice to file anything he wants" (quoted in O'Brien 2017, 287).[2] When he retired in 1975, Justice Douglas had authored 648 dissents—still the highest total of any justice in history.

The 1970s saw the development of another set of important institutional developments that transformed the Court and served to solidify minority coalitions and undermine consensus. First, in 1971, the Court added a syllabus to each opinion. For the first time, each justice's vote was visible in every case, adding pressure to rationalize a dissent with a written opinion. The practice of notation, where a justice would simply note a dissent at the end of majority opinion rather than issue a written dissenting opinion, as in "Justice Douglas dissents," largely ended (see Fife et al. 2017). Justice William Brennan explained his concerns with the practice of notation: "[W]here significant and deeply held disagreement exists, members of the Court have a responsibility to articulate it. This is why, when I dissent, I always say why I am doing so. Simply to say, 'I dissent,' I will not do" (1986, 435). Second, the number of law clerks doubled, then tripled, and they took on the primary responsibility for drafting opinions, including dissents (Ward and Weiden 2006; Peppers and Ward 2012).

Third, and most important, formalized dissent assignment practices began. The most senior justice in the dissenting coalition would formally assign the principal dissent author, and members of the dissent coalition had to decide whether to join the principal dissent, draft their own dissents, or both (Cook 1995). During earlier eras, justices were either not particularly interested in expressing their own views on some matters or were loath to expend resources drafting dissenting opinions. But once dissents were formally assigned, a justice's existing workload was taken into consideration by the senior justice responsible for the assignment. Assignees felt more collegial pressure to write than they had before.

While some dissent assigning behavior took place among some justices prior to the 1970s, it was during the Burger Court that the practice became formalized. An example of dissent assignment is *Foremost Insurance Co. v. Richardson* (1982), where Justice Lewis Powell's clerk Mary Becker wrote her justice: "I am unconvinced by Justice Marshall's opinion. . . . You are the senior justice in dissent! Justices Rehnquist and O'Connor also dissented in a 6–3 vote. Should we write or assign?"[3]

Justice Brennan is primarily responsible for the practice of dissent assignment (Cook 1995). He always assigned the dissent when he was the senior member of the minority coalition, a position he was often in after Justice Douglas's retirement in 1975. Even when Justice Brennan was not in dissent, he would encourage the senior member of the dissenting coalition to make the assignment. Chief Justices Warren Burger and William Rehnquist followed Brennan's lead and assigned dissents when they were in the minority.

Not unlike chief justices, Justice Brennan had three priorities when making dissent assignments (Cook 1995). First, he considered workload, not only outstanding dissents that his colleagues were working on but also the majority opinions they had been assigned. Next, he valued expertise, choosing justices who had a particular background or interest in a given issue. For example, in *Dow Chemical Co. v. United States* (1986) Justice Powell wrote to Justice Brennan: "This is merely to say that unless you wish to write the dissents in these cases, I would be happy to take them. I think our views coincide very closely. And, after all, certainly you and I know more about reconnaissance aircraft . . . than some of our other friends!"[4] Justice Brennan assigned the principal dissent to Justice Powell. Beverly Blair Cook (1995) also noted that Justice Brennan chose ideologically distant justices whenever possible. Sandra L. Wood and Gary M. Gansle (1997) confirmed these findings as did Saul Brenner and Harold J. Spaeth (1988), with the caveat that in decisions where one vote could have changed the outcome (e.g., 5–4 decisions), the dissent was instead authored by the marginal, or most ideologically moderate, justice in the coalition. It is plain that Justice Brennan's strategy in narrowly divided cases was to choose the justice most likely to write an opinion that might siphon off a vote from the majority coalition and therefore potentially turn the minority into the majority.

It is important to note that dissent assignments were different in form than majority assignments. Whereas majority assignments were treated as orders, dissent assignments were considered requests that might be declined. In her study of dissent assignment practices, Cook finds that "dissent assignments . . . do not carry the same authority [as majority opinion assignments]; they are couched in a language of collegiality rather than of hierarchy. Seniors address their juniors with circumspection in making dissent assignments. . . . Justices treat the letter from their senior in dissent as an invitation, not an order, and immediately respond" (1995, 23). For example, Justice Brennan wrote Justice Byron White: "I've been trying to whack up the accumulating dissents. Would . . . *Ingraham v. Wright* (you, John [Paul Stevens] and I are in dissent) and . . . *Vendo Co. v. Lektro-Vend Corp.* (you, Thurgood [Marshall], John and I are in dissent) interest you?"[5] Similarly, in *Crawford Fitting Co. v. J. T. Gibbons* (1987), Justice Brennan wrote Justice Marshall: "You and I are in dissent (so what else is new?). Will you, Thurgood, try your hand at it?"[6]

However, some justices viewed the assignment of dissents more formally: In *Interstate Commerce Commission v. American Trucking Association* (1984), Justice Harry Blackmun wrote Justice Sandra O'Connor: "You, Lewis [Powell], John [Stevens], and I are in dissent in this case. It is early for me to do this, but I wondered whether you would be willing to undertake the dissent. It seemed to me that you had the issues very well in mind."[7] Justice O'Connor answered: "I would prefer to wait until the assignments are made before deciding whether to take on another dissent, if that is all right as far as you are concerned."[8] Justice Blackmun responded: "Your note of this morning prompts me to be perfectly candid. I have the assignment power for the dissent in this case and in due course I propose to exercise it. I doubt that you are any more burdened with respect to majorities and dissents than any of the rest of us."[9] Justice O'Connor then replied: "If your assignment offer is still open for the dissent in this case I would be happy to try to draft one." She also added a handwritten note at the bottom of the memo: "P.S. Harry, thank you again for correcting my unfortunate misunderstanding of our informal practice in this regard."[10]

With the explosion of law clerks to do the writing, justices generally agreed to dissent assignments. It was only on rare occasions that a justice declined a dissent assignment, either due to the time pressures or uncertainty about the case. For example, in *County of Washington, Oregon v. Gunther* (1981), Chief Justice Burger initially asked Justice Potter Stewart, but Justice Stewart expressed uncertainty in how he would ultimately vote: "At the Conference discussion of this case, it became evident to me that at least some members of the majority did not see it as involving the broad and important issues that I perceived. . . . I would prefer to wait to see what the Court is going to say, and may well end up by joining the Court opinion."[11] Similarly, Justice Brennan initially asked then-Associate Justice Rehnquist to draft the dissent in *Japan Whaling Assn. v. American Cetacean Society* (1986). Justice Rehnquist responded: "As you will recall, I passed at Conference on this case and later tentatively voted to affirm. My views are still so unsettled—and very likely at least partially at odds with those expressed by the other dissenters at Conference—that I would prefer not to undertake the dissent in this case."[12] Justice Rehnquist ultimately joined Justice Marshall's principal dissent.

During this period, dissents increasingly emerged during majority coalition formation when members of the original majority could not reach agreement with their colleagues and defected to the minority. This was the case in *Lugar v. Edmondson Oil* (1982), when both Justice Powell and Justice O'Connor circulated concurrences but could not reach agreement with the others in the majority and subsequently dissented. Justice Powell wrote his clerk Dick Fallon: "Now that we know that BRW [Byron R. White]'s opinion will become a Court opinion, I think it necessary to rewrite our opinion. As a dissenting opinion, it should confront the Court's opinion as strongly as we can without being strident. I have never been more convinced that a majority of the Justices were 'dead wrong.' . . . I therefore view our dissent as important for the long term."[13] Justice O'Connor joined Justice Powell's dissent and wrote him: "I really like the new dissent. The Court's opinion is perhaps one of the most unfortunate of the entire Term. How I wish we could swing another vote your way!"[14]

The Court today reflects the imprint of these crucial institutional changes in both formal processes and informal norms. While the early days of the Court are known for high levels of consensus and the practice of acquiescence, it was also during those early years that the first dissent-incentivizing reforms were introduced. Chief Justice Marshall's push to issue "Opinion of the Court" was coupled with the practice of identifying which justice authored the opinion. The unintended consequence of identifying the author of the majority opinion was to now make justices much more attentive to what positions were attached to them, and the implications of more publicly and individually taking those positions. The norm of acquiescence faltered, and one of individual expression grew. Dissent blocs began to form, with increased consultation among the dissenters, and justices increasingly publicly defended the use of dissents. By the time the syllabus was introduced in 1971, as well as the practice of formalized dissent assignments, a culture of dissent flourished on the Court, one that continues unabated today. In the next section, we examine why (and when) justices dissent in the modern era.

Why (and When) Justices Dissent in the Modern Era

From 1953 to 2004, the proportion of Supreme Court decisions with at least one dissenting opinion was 0.614 (Epstein et al. 2007). What factors influence a justice's decision to dissent? Building on our previous work that focused on what leads the Court to issue unanimous opinions (Corley, Steigerwalt, and Ward 2013), we apply our theoretical framework for understanding judicial behavior to the question of individual dissenting behavior. Previous scholars provide different explanations for dissents, with a primary focus on ideological considerations, strategic factors, and the institutional context in which justices act (see, e.g., Wahlbeck, Spriggs, and Maltzman 1999; Bryan and Ringsmuth 2016). We argue that these factors need to be considered as operating in tandem, rather than as individual, discrete forces. More importantly, we further propose that legal considerations may constrain or enable ideological voting and, consequently, may influence whether a justice votes to dissent from the majority opinion. We previously found that, at the aggregate level, dissensus was more likely in cases where legal certainty is low (Corley, Steigerwalt, and Ward 2013). We therefore now investigate the influence of legal certainty through our model of individual dissenting behavior.

Our comprehensive model of individual dissenting behavior begins by recognizing the strong influence of justices' personal policy preferences in conjunction with the particular facts of the case being decided (Segal and Spaeth 2002). The decision to dissent fundamentally stems from a justice's disagreement with the majority opinion (see, e.g., Wahlbeck, Spriggs, and Maltzman 1999; Epstein, Landes, and Posner 2011; Bryan and Ringsmuth 2016). Not surprisingly, dissenting justices are usually ideologically distant from the majority coalition and/or the majority opinion author, using dissents to publicly air these differences (see e.g., Wahlbeck, Spriggs, and Maltzman 1999). Pritchett's (1945) analysis of the 1943–44 term identifies ideologically aligned voting blocs that help explain some of the dissent patterns that emerged that year, offering one of the first suggestions that dissents may reflect ideological disagreement. Neal Devins and Lawrence Baum (2016) build on these findings and others to argue that the current Court reflects the increasing party polarization gripping the nation; they propose that changing elite legal socialization and social network norms and judicial confirmation practices ensure the Court will increasingly reflect the country's partisan divisions. We therefore expect that a justice is more likely to dissent when that justice is ideologically distant from the majority opinion writer.

However, while justices wish to see their personal policy preferences enacted into law, justices are not unconstrained actors. "Rather, justices are strategic actors who realize that their ability to achieve their goals depends on a consideration of the preference of other actors, the choices they expect others to make, and the institutional context in which they act" (Epstein and Knight 1998, 10). The Supreme Court is a collegial decision-making body, and seeing one's preferences enacted into law requires a justice to gain support from her colleagues. Justices may therefore join a majority opinion with the hopes of narrowing its reach and blunting its impact. Justices are also concerned about the role of the Court in the larger national policymaking arena. They may therefore suppress their desire to dissent in certain cases, such as those in which they are concerned with maintaining the legitimacy of the Court.[15]

To test for the influence of strategic considerations, we take into account whether the majority opinion is reversing precedent or overturning a statute. On the one hand, scholars argue that when the Court overturns existing precedent or declares a federal, state, or municipal law unconstitutional, it is behaving as an "activist" Court (Keck 2004; Pickerill 2004). Because they are directly invalidating the actions of other political actors—and in some cases the will of the people—the justices often discuss the propriety of speaking with one institutional voice in an attempt to enhance the decision's legitimacy. Thus, justices may be more hesitant to dissent in these types of cases.

On the other hand, since exercising judicial review and overruling prior precedent are actions the Court does not take lightly, it may be harder for individual justices to suppress their desire to dissent. In fact, Paul H. Edelman, David E. Klein, and Stefanie A. Lindquist (2012) argue that overruling precedent is a "dramatic doctrinal step [that is more likely] in cases where justices feel especially strongly about the policy issues involved" (140). As a result, justices may be more likely to vote ideologically—and thus more likely to dissent when they disagree with the majority opinion—in a case where the majority is overruling precedent instead of upholding it. Similarly, Brian R. Sala and James F. Spriggs II (2004) find that, contrary to their expectations, decisions by the Court to strike down statutes are best predicted by ideological rather than strategic motivations. For these reasons, we control for whether the Court overturned an existing precedent or struck down a statute as unconstitutional, but we do not make a prediction as to the direction of the effect such an action may have on a justice's decision to dissent.

Our model of dissent also accounts for the unique institutional role of the chief justice in potentially suppressing dissent. First, if the chief justice is in the majority, he has the power to assign the majority opinion. We propose that one way chief justices may leverage their institutional role to encourage consensus is by strategically utilizing their power of self-assignment. By self-assigning the majority opinion, chiefs can ensure that the opinion is written in such a way that guards against other justices defecting and voting to dissent (Epstein and Knight 1998; Wahlbeck 2006). Thus, we expect that if the chief justice authors the opinion, justices are less likely to dissent.

Similarly, chief justices, given their distinctive institutional position on the Court, may be more concerned than other justices with producing larger majority opinions as a bulwark against public backlash. For example, as an associate justice, Rehnquist joined several majority opinions carving out exceptions to the *Miranda* rule such as threats to public safety (*New York v. Quarles,* 1984). As chief justice, however, Rehnquist capitulated and joined the majority in *Dickerson v. United States* (2000) to uphold *Miranda*. Chief Justice Rehnquist's former law clerk and successor as chief justice, John Roberts, explained how *Miranda* exemplified Rehnquist's changing role from associate justice to chief justice: "He appreciated that it had become part of the law—that it would do more harm to uproot it—and he wrote that opinion as chief for the good of the institution" (Rosen 2007). Thus, the chief justice may join the majority opinion even when he disagrees with it, suppressing his dissent. According to Frank B. Cross and Stefanie A. Lindquist (2006), "the position of Chief Justice may produce 'golden shackles' that limit the Chief's individual freedom. . . . The Chief may have to compromise her preferences in order to build a greater majority or control the assignment of the opinion" (1678). This leads us to hypothesize that chief justices are less likely to dissent than their colleagues.

Collegiality is another strategic consideration that may influence whether a justice votes to dissent. Rachael K. Hinkle, Morgan Hazelton, and Michael J.

Nelson (2017) find that as the number of terms two justices serve together on the Court increases, the likelihood of dissent decreases. They argue that as justices serve together longer on the Court, they become more familiar with each other, and this continuing relationship increases their ability to reach agreement because the potential dissenter is able to bargain with the majority opinion author. However, Amanda C. Bryan and Eve M. Ringsmuth (2016, 169) argue and find the exact opposite. They instead posit that the longer justices serve together, the more they can trust that collegial relationship will continue even if they disagree on certain cases. We therefore control for the number of years the potential dissenter and the majority opinion author have served on the Court together, but we do not make a prediction as to the direction of the effect that familiarity may have on the justice's decision to dissent.

Another factor that may influence whether a justice dissents is how long the justice has served on the Court. Scholars often argue that justices experience a "freshman effect," with new justices taking a few years to assimilate and become comfortable in their new job (see, e.g., Wahlbeck, Spriggs, and Maltzman 1999; Bryan and Ringsmuth 2016). Marcus E. Hendershot and colleagues (2013) find evidence that justices are more likely to dissent the longer they serve on the Court, suggesting pressures to compromise work most forcefully during a justice's early tenure. This means that early in their tenure, justices may suppress their dissent in order to avoid conflict and develop collegial relationships with their colleagues, but these suppression effects wane the longer they sit on the bench. Accordingly, we expect that the longer the justice has served on the Court, the more likely the justice will dissent.

We also explore whether case factors have a relationship with a justice's decision to dissent. Certain cases, because of the issues they deal with, may be more likely to fuel dissents. Ideological preferences on civil liberties may be more defined and deeply held than those on other issues. Scholars find that civil liberties cases are less likely to be decided unanimously than other types of cases (see, e.g., Hensley and Johnson 1998; Hurwitz and Lanier 2004; Corley, Steigerwalt, and Ward 2013). Additionally, Isaac Unah and Ange-Marie Hancock (2006) and Brandon Bartels (2011) find that issue salience intensifies the impact of ideology on case outcomes, thereby decreasing the likelihood of dissent suppression. Thus, we expect that justices will be more likely to dissent in cases involving civil rights and liberties.

Cases with a high degree of salience to external political actors and the public are salient to the justices as well and therefore may be more likely to expose divisions among them. In a nonsalient case, alternatively, justices may be willing to suppress their dissents. We therefore expect that justices will be more likely to dissent in politically salient cases.

Finally, our model of dissenting behavior extends beyond the attitudinal and strategic factors outlined above to also consider the role of legal forces on the decision of whether or not to dissent. In previous work (Corley, Steigerwalt, and Ward 2013), we argue and find that legal forces, and specifically the level of legal certainty in a case, influence whether the Supreme Court is able to achieve unanimous decisions. As Lawrence Baum (1997) notes, "The easy case gives precedence to legal considerations, because judges are directed to the result that has greater legal support. From the perspective of motivated reasoning, judges are unlikely to reach a decision consistent with their policy preferences when they would have great difficulty justifying it in legal terms" (66). We build on this argument to propose that justices will be cognizant of the level of "legal certainty" in a particular case. Our concept of "legal certainty" captures the notion that the justices are presented with signals in each case about the degree to which the law and facts point to a single legal answer as opposed to multiple potential legal interpretations. We look to signals received by the justices prior to the case being heard to create our novel legal certainty scale (Corley, Steigerwalt, and Ward 2013). Low levels of legal certainty reflect cases where there is no clear legal answer, equally plausible answers exist on both sides, and the constraining power of the law is consequently minimized. In contrast, high levels of legal certainty occur in cases where the relevant information and signals suggest there is a single, mutually agreeable answer.

Our earlier work demonstrates that legal certainty helps explain when unanimity is most likely to occur: unanimity is most likely when the level of legal certainty is high, and least likely when it is low. This earlier work focused on the decisions of the Court as a whole, and so we extend the reasoning here to the decisions of individual justices. We argue that the level of legal certainty in a case influences the ability of a justice's preferences to predominate. In cases with low levels of legal certainty in which many potential legal answers abound, the justice has an opportunity to vote according to her personal policy preferences. In contrast, cases with high levels of legal certainty constrain the justice's ability to vote for anything but a single legal answer. Thus, we expect that justices will be more likely to dissent when the level of legal certainty in a case is low and less likely to dissent when the level of legal certainty is high.

Data and Methods

To conduct the analysis in this chapter, we focus on all federal circuit court cases that were granted certiorari, orally argued, and decided by the Court during the 1953–2004 terms,[16] using the Supreme Court database (Spaeth et al. 2021). Since our interest is in explaining the individual justice's decision to dissent, we identified whether each justice (other than the majority opinion author) voted to dissent, and thus our unit of analysis is the justice-vote. The dependent variable is coded 1 if the justice voted to dissent, and 0 otherwise. We account for the possibility that variance in dissenting might be due to shifts over time, and that certain justices may be more likely to dissent than others, by estimating a multilevel model with random effects for term and justice. Specifically, the justice is nested within the Court's annual terms. Since the dependent variable is dichotomous, we use a multilevel probit model.

We operationalize each of our independent variables in the following manner:

Ideological Distance between Justice and Majority Opinion Author. To measure a justice's ideological distance from the majority opinion author (MOA), we use Segal-Cover scores to measure ideology (Segal and Cover 1989) and then calculate the absolute value of the difference between the two justices. We use Segal-Cover scores for this analysis since it is derived not from the justices' votes but rather external assessments of justice ideology; this allays any endogeneity concerns since we are interested in explaining justices' votes. This variable ranges from 0 to 1 with a mean of 0.314 and standard deviation of 0.256.

Altered Precedent/Law Declared Unconstitutional. Using the Spaeth dataset, this variable is a categorical variable measured as 1 if a case formally alters precedent or declares an act of Congress unconstitutional, and 0 otherwise. This variable takes on a value of 1 in 6.74 percent of our observations.

Chief Justice. There are two variables related to the influence of the chief justice: whether the chief justice wrote the majority opinion and whether the chief justice is the justice deciding whether or not to dissent. If the chief justice wrote the majority opinion, the variable is coded 1, 0 otherwise. The chief justice wrote the majority opinion in 10.44 percent of the observations. If the justice deciding whether or not to dissent is the chief justice, the variable is coded 1, and 0 otherwise.

Cotenure. To control for cotenure (joint years of service on the bench), we count the number of years the justice and majority opinion author have served together at the time of the relevant case. This variable ranges from 0 to 32, with a mean of 7.4 and standard deviation of 5.83.

Years on the Court. In order to account for a possible "freshman effect," we count the number of years the justice has been on the Court at the time of the relevant case. This variable ranges from 0 to 36, with a mean of 12.43 and standard deviation of 8.68.

Issue Salience. We created a dummy variable for whether the case concerns a civil liberties or rights issue. This variable takes on the value of 1 in 46.44 percent of the observations.

Political Salience. We measure political salience as cases covered on the front page of the *New York Times* the day after the decision is announced (Epstein and Segal 2000).[17] Salient cases are coded 1, and nonsalient cases are coded 0. This variable takes on the value of 1 in 15.44 percent of observations.

Level of Legal Certainty. In our previous work (Corley, Steigerwalt, and Ward 2013), we measured legal certainty by creating an index based on the following five discrete variables: legally noncomplex cases, lack of amicus participation in the case, lack of legal conflict, lack of legal dissensus in the lower court, and statutory interpretation. Each of these five variables was coded dichotomously, with each variable coded such that 1 signals a higher level of legal certainty. We then simply added these five variables to create our index, scaled from 0 to 5, with 0 reflecting the lowest possible level of legal certainty and 5 representing the highest. In our data, the mean level of legal certainty is 3.37 with a standard deviation of 1.02.

Results

Table 1 displays the parameter estimates for our model, indicating which factors increase or decrease the likelihood of a justice voting to dissent. The likelihood ratio test shows that the random intercept model is statistically superior to the probit model, and that in order to correctly test our hypotheses of interest, we need to account for the variance that exists both over time and between different justices. Overall, the results show that our theory of dissents helps to explain when dissents are most and least likely to occur.

As expected, the results show that a justice is more likely to dissent when the justice and the majority opinion author ideologically disagree. The baseline predicted probability of a justice voting to dissent, setting all continuous independent variables at their means and all dichotomous independent variables at their modes, is 0.177. The likelihood of a justice dissenting increases by 15.82 percent (0.177 to 0.205) when the ideological difference between the majority opinion author and the justice increases from its mean to one standard deviation above the mean; the likelihood of dissenting decreases by 14.12 percent (0.177 to 0.152) when the ideological distance between the majority opinion author and the potential dissenter decreases from its mean to one standard deviation below the mean. Figure 2 graphically illustrates the relationship between ideological disagreement and the probability of dissent.

Table 1 provides support for the argument that the chief justice's institutional role influences dissenting behavior on the Court. When the chief justice is the majority opinion author, the predicted probability of one of his colleagues voting to dissent decreases from 0.177 to 0.151, a decrease of 14.69 percent. This finding suggests that chiefs can use their institutional power of self-assignment to encourage consensus and suppress dissents. And when the chief justice is making the decision whether or not to dissent, he is

TABLE 1. Multi-Level probit model with random effects for justice and term: Whether justice votes to dissent, 1953–2004

Variable	Coefficient	S.E.	p-value
Ideological difference between justice and MOA	0.398	0.037	0.000
Altered precedent/declared statute unconstitutional	0.012	0.033	0.707
Chief Justice Writes Majority Opinion	-0.106	0.028	0.000
Chief Justice Votes	-0.270	0.049	0.000
Years of Joint Service (between Justice and MOA)	0.004	0.002	0.024
Years on the Court	0.014	0.001	0.000
Civil liberties or rights issue	0.153	0.017	0.000
Politically salient case	0.193	0.022	0.000
Level of legal certainty	-0.039	0.009	0.000
Constant	-5.641	1.440	0.000
Variance Components			
Term-level	0.008	0.004	--
Justice-level	0.074	0.008	--

N = 32,728; p-values based on two-tailed tests.
LR test vs. probit model: chi2(2) = 624.27; Prob > chi2 = 0.000.

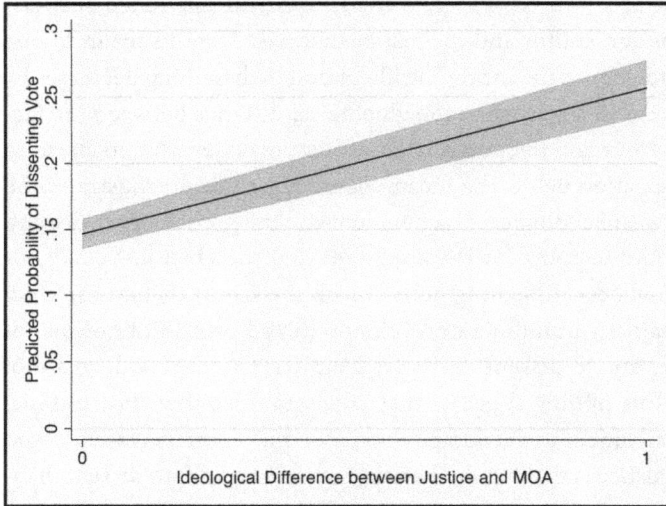

FIGURE 2. Probability of justice voting to dissent in relation to ideological difference between justice and majority opinion author

less likely to dissent compared to the other justices on the Court, with the predicted probability of the chief justice dissenting 0.116 compared to 0.177, a decrease of 34.46 percent. Figures 3 and 4 graphically display these relationships.

We next examine the extent to which familiarity with the other justices and the Court influence a justice's decision to dissent. First, we find that as the number of years the justice and the majority opinion author have served together at the time of the relevant case increases—their cotenure—the justice is more likely to dissent. Figure 5 shows the predicted probability of dissenting over the values in the dataset. The predicted probability of dissent increases by a modest 3.39 percent (from 0.177 to 0.183) when the number of years the justice and the majority opinion author have served together increases from its mean to one standard deviation above the mean. The effect of cotenure grows, however, when justices serve together for considerable periods of time: when either justice is new to the bench, the predicted probability of dissenting is 0.170; when cotenure is set to its maximum value, indicating that the justices have served together on the bench for thirty-two years, the predicted probability jumps to 0.204, an increase of 20 percent. As Bryan and Ringsmuth (2016, 169) argue, the more justices interact with their colleagues, the more they trust their collegiality.[18]

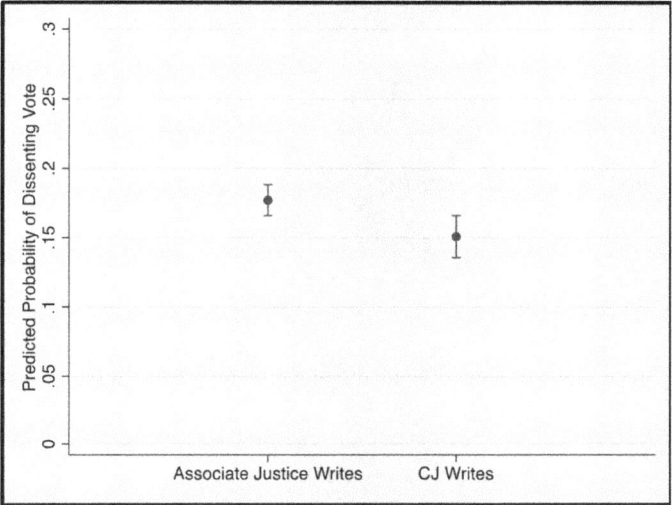

FIGURE 3. Probability of justice voting to dissent when chief justice writes majority opinion

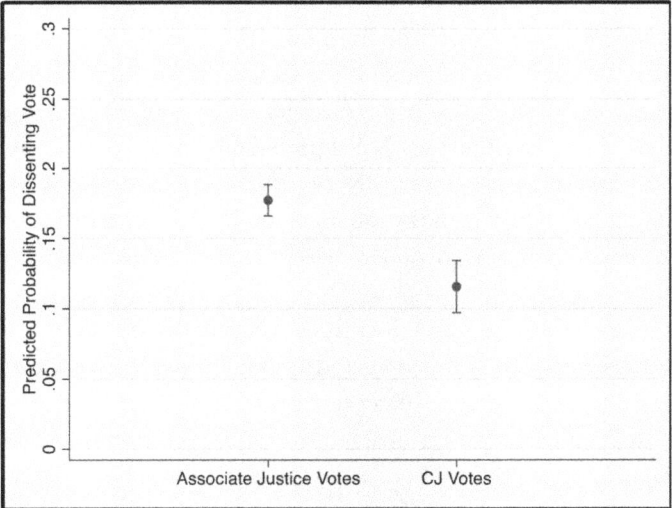

FIGURE 4. Probability of chief justice voting to dissent

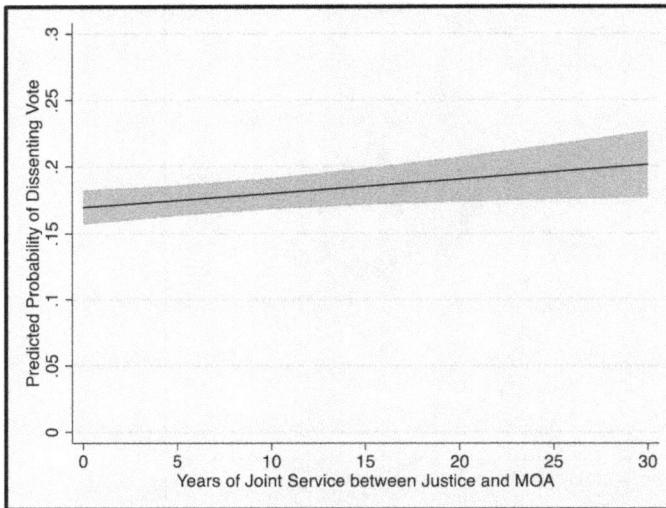

FIGURE 5. Probability of justice voting to dissent in relation to years of joint service with majority opinion author

Similarly, the longer a justice serves on the Court, the more likely a justice will vote to dissent. When a justice first joins the Court, the predicted probability of dissenting is 0.137; when the justice has served for a number of years (one standard deviation above the mean), that probability increases to 0.209, a 52.55 percent increase. Figure 6 graphically depicts this relationship. These findings suggest that familiarity with the job increases justices' comfort level with voting according to their sincere preferences instead of suppressing their dissents.

Salient cases are more likely to result in a justice voting to dissent compared with nonsalient cases. Specifically, the predicted probability of a justice voting to dissent increases by 31.07 percent (0.177 to 0.232) for a salient case compared to a nonsalient one. In addition, civil liberties and rights cases—those we predicted would be most divisive because of the issues they involve—are indeed more likely to lead to a justice voting to dissent than other types of cases, with the predicted probability increasing by 24.29 percent (an increase from 0.177 to 0.220). The broader implication is that the types of the cases the Court elects to hear can influence whether dissensual behavior will emerge. When the Court selects a docket filled with civil liberties cases, or those of high external salience, dissents are more likely to emerge. Alternatively, the

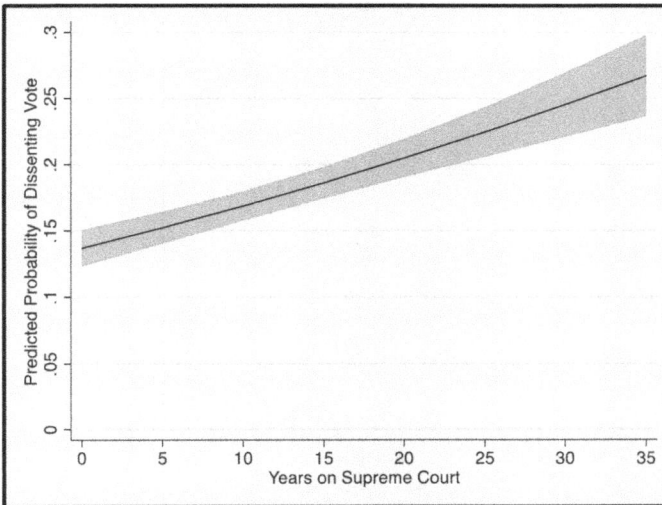

FIGURE 6. Probability of justice voting to dissent in relation to years served on Supreme Court

rate of dissent may decrease if the Court elects to hear cases raising other, equally important but less outwardly divisive legal questions. Figures 7 and 8 graphically display these relationships.

Finally, building on our earlier work (Corley, Steigerwalt, and Ward 2013), our results showcase the importance of accounting for the influence of legal forces and constraints on an individual justice's decision making. When investigating the role legal certainty plays in the dissenting behavior of the justices, we find that as the level of legal certainty in a case increases, the likelihood of a justice voting to dissent decreases. Figure 9 shows the predicted probability of dissenting over the values in the dataset. Specifically, when the level of legal certainty is set to 0, indicating a low level of legal certainty, the predicted probability of a justice dissenting is 0.213. When the level of legal certainty is set to 5, indicating a high level of legal certainty, the predicted probability of a justice dissenting decreases to 0.161, a decrease of 24.41 percent. Legal forces, and particularly the level of legal certainty in a case, can both enable and undermine the ability of dissent to emerge. When the evidence and signals available to the justices point toward a single legal answer, the likelihood of an individual justice dissenting diminishes. Our results thus illuminate that while justices seek to see their personal policy preferences enshrined into law,

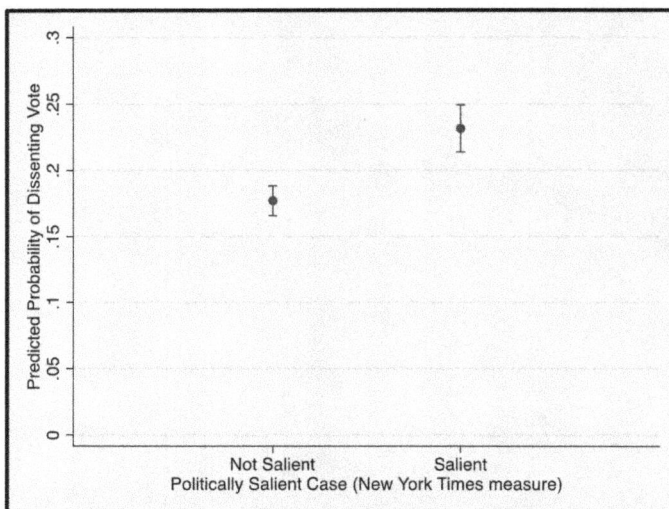

FIGURE 7. Probability of justice voting to dissent in relation to political salience of case

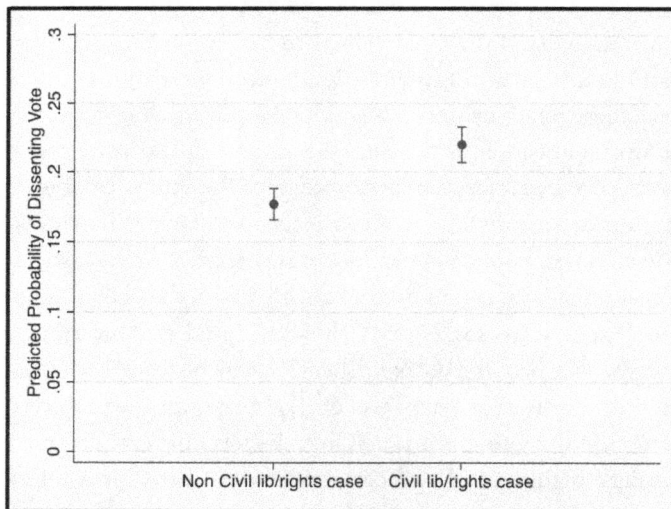

FIGURE 8. Probability of justice voting to dissent in relation to type of issue

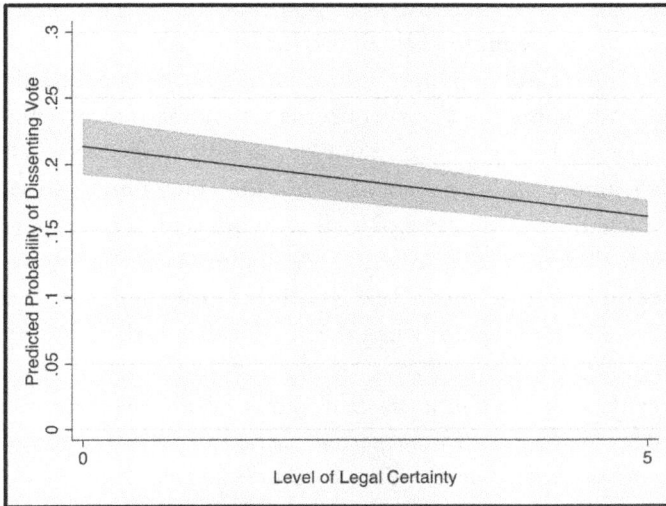

FIGURE 9. Probability of justice voting to dissent in relation to level of legal certainty of the case

sometimes the law itself is simply not amenable to this goal. And these findings showcase the importance of taking into consideration all potential influences on the justices' votes, including potential legal constraints. While the law may at times be malleable or open to multiple interpretations, at other times the law offers only a single answer to the important legal question at hand.

Conclusion

In this chapter, we seek to explain how the modern era of dissensus arrived as well as why (and when) justices dissent in the modern era. Our historical assessment of formal and informal institutional changes reveals that the Court has adopted a number of practices and procedures that aid the airing of dissent. From a growing concern with individual consistency to the elimination of the Court's mandatory docket to the adoption of the case syllabus and more formalized dissent assignment practices, today's Court operates in a structural environment designed to encourage and enable individual expression.

But when are individual justices most likely to dissent? We offer a theory of dissenting behavior that recognizes the numerous factors that combine to influence justices' voting decisions. Overall, we find that this theory helps to explain dissenting behavior: dissents are a function of multiple, concurrently operating forces. Justices are more likely to dissent when they are ideologically distant from the majority opinion author, when the case is politically salient, when the case before the Court concerns a civil liberties or rights issue, when the justices have served on the Court a long time, and when they have served with the majority opinion author for a long time. Justices are less likely to dissent when the level of legal certainty is high, suggesting that cases in which a stronger legal answer exists suppresses dissenting behavior. Finally, we find that chief justices are less likely to vote to dissent and that a justice is less likely to dissent when the chief justice is the majority opinion author.

Taken together, these results illuminate that justices will dissent to express their personal policy views, but also that certain cases, and certain contexts, aid justices in doing so. On the one hand, newer justices and chief justices are less likely than their colleagues to dissent; justices are also less likely to dissent from one another when they have served together for only a short period of time. These acclimation and collegiality effects suggest justices build up both experience and collegial trust over the years; when both are high, dissent is more likely. Alternatively, the chief's unique institutional position leads him to dissent less frequently than his colleagues, perhaps as a mechanism to encourage broader consensus on the Court. On the other hand, justices feel enabled to dissent in those cases that also divide the elected branches and the public. Politically salient cases and civil liberties cases are the most likely to garner outside attention, and are also those where dissent is more likely as compared to nonsalient and non–civil liberties cases.

Perhaps most notably, legal considerations also play an important role in dissent behavior. Extending our previous work, and in stark contrast to most analyses of justice voting behavior, we find that not only is the Court as an institution influenced by legal certainty, but so too are individual justices. When legal considerations are most apparent, and the level of legal certainty in a case is high, individual justices are less likely to dissent; when legal certainty is low, dissent appears more readily. The implication is that even individual dissenting behavior is potentially constrained by legal, institutional, and strategic forces, as well as a desire to see one's personal policy preferences embedded in the law. Our results also suggest future models of judicial decision-making need to account for all potential influences, including legal forces, in order to accurately capture why justices vote the way they do.

Once justices decide to dissent, the next stage of the process is to try to build a dissent coalition. What does the dissent coalition negotiation and bargaining process look like? Does it operate much like the majority opinion coalition-building process, or does it have its own distinct character? In the next chapter, we offer the first ever assessment of dissent coalition-building behavior, based on the papers of Justices Powell and Blackmun.

2 | Endeavoring to Accommodate

Dissent Coalition Behavior

THE JUSTICES OF the US Supreme Court are engaged in an ongoing and spirited legal and policy dialogue with other political actors, the public, and their fellow justices. As we explained in the introduction, this book focuses on the justices' dialogue with each other. What does this conversation look like? And how can we begin to understand what portions of this internal debate become part of the public record?

An important component of this internal dialogue is the disagreements that exist among the justices, and how these disagreements may—or may not—become formal, public dissents. In the preceding chapter, we explored both the Supreme Court's transformation from an entity of consensus to an arena of dissensus as well as why justices ultimately decide to dissent in certain cases. In this chapter we investigate what comes after justices decide to dissent: the dissent coalition formation and bargaining process. While there are a number of studies that specifically address majority coalition bargaining and accommodation, including attempts by the majority opinion writer and others to forestall potential dissents (see, e.g., Maltzman, Spriggs, and Wahlbeck 2000), relatively little is known about the process of bargaining and accommodation that occurs among justices in the minority.

The publication of a dissent is a formal acknowledgment that bargaining and accommodation between the justices has broken down. Dissenters hope to provoke the majority into responding to them in the majority opinion, ensuring their views become part of the legal and policy dialogue. But what does the discourse between the potential dissenting justices look like? This chapter examines this important question. We provide one of the first investigations, based on the papers of Justices Lewis Powell and Harry Blackmun, of the internal deliberations that ultimately result in a formal dissent, or even multiple dissents. This assessment will aid us in better understanding both the justices' discussions, as well as how these dissent coalition debates may ultimately influence which dissents the majority will highlight, enshrining these dissents more firmly in the national legal and policy debate.

Bargaining and Accommodation on the Court: A First Look at Dissent Coalition Negotiations

Several major studies explore bargaining and accommodation among majority-coalition justices (see, e.g., Murphy 1964; Epstein and Knight 1998; Maltzman, Spriggs, and Wahlbeck 2000). They argue that justices act rationally and strategically to achieve their policy preferences by considering the positions of their colleagues. According to Forrest Maltzman, James F. Spriggs II, and Paul J. Wahlbeck (2000): "To achieve policy outcomes as close as possible to their own preferences, justices must at a minimum take into account the choices made by their colleagues, with whom they ultimately must negotiate, bargain, and compromise" (16–17).

In his landmark study of judicial strategy, Walter F. Murphy (1964) finds "recurrent and rather consistent patterns of negotiation and bargaining within the Court" (198). Majority coalition justices negotiate to ensure their positions are accurately included in the final opinion of the Court. The majority opinion author must traverse a rocky path as she attempts to accommodate various potentially distinctive or even differing arguments while also holding together the majority:

> The Justice who has been assigned the task of writing the opinion of the Court may see himself a broker adjusting the interests of his associates as well as of himself. His problems, of course, are dynamic rather than static. By making a change in an opinion to pick up one vote he may lose another. Moreover, by compromising and incorporating several different lines of reasoning in his opinion he may expose himself to even more damaging dissent. . . . Most important, a Justice would want to avoid having to water down his policy to the point where it ceased to be an operational doctrine—though it is possible that emasculation may be the only alternative to an outright rejection of his policy by the majority. (Murphy 1964, 64)

For other members of the Court, "The most significant items a Justice has to offer in trade are his vote and his concurrence in an opinion. Conversely . . . threats to change a vote or to write a separate opinion, dissenting or concurring, are the sanctions most generally available to a Justice. When the Court is sharply divided any Justice can wield great influence" (Murphy 1964, 57). Yet even a highly consensual coalition, for example an initial eight-justice majority, may seek even greater consensus by using institutional arguments to gain the votes of solo dissenters. "In situations where the Justice feels that the general political environment requires unanimity, he might play on the isolation of a would-be dissenter" (Murphy 1964, 46).

Maltzman, Spriggs, and Wahlbeck (2000) build on Murphy's work through an examination of Justice William Brennan's papers and his extensive records of internal Court negotiations and draft opinions. They find that the majority opinion author is most open to negotiation while the majority coalition is being formed; once the opinion author secures five votes, the potential for bargaining and compromise decreases precipitously. Justice Brennan's records reveal that a justice sent a note to the majority opinion author recommending a specific change in 23.4 percent (527 of the 2,295) of signed opinions or assigned cases during the Burger Court (1969–86).

Pamela C. Corley (2010) provides additional insight into bargaining and accommodation on the Supreme Court as it relates to concurrences. She examined the private papers of Justices Harry A. Blackmun and Thurgood Marshall during the 1986 to 1989 terms. Corley finds that out of fifty-five majority opinions written by Justice Blackmun, thirty-one (56%) contained at least one bargaining statement from another justice, and that Justice Blackmun subsequently revised the majority opinion in response to these bargaining statements in twenty-eight cases (90%). Of the cases where Justice Blackmun did make some sort of accommodation, in only six (21%) did a published concurrence still emerge. Justice Marshall wrote fifty-eight majority opinions during these terms and thirty-seven (64%) contained at least one bargaining statement from another justice; Justice Marshall at least partially accommodated his brethren in thirty (81%) of these cases. Corley's investigation reveals that solely examining the final opinions and votes obscures the crucial deliberations that take place along the way, some of which may change the ultimate outcomes.

What has yet to be explored is what this bargaining and negotiation process looks like from the perspective of the dissent coalition. In this chapter, we use the papers of Justices Blackmun and Powell to investigate deliberations within the dissenting coalition itself. Each of the justice's papers were examined for records of dissent coalition formation and bargaining. We focused primarily on records of letters and memos sent between the justices on specific cases. This theory-generating exploration focused on identifying instances of dissent coalition discussions within these letters and memos, and then assessing the content of those discussions: What did the justices discuss with each other? Did they seek to convince others to join the dissent coalition? If so, what tactics were used? Did they debate goals or strategies? Were these dissent coalition discussions mainly about opinion content or did the justices focus on other aspects of the negotiation and bargaining process? These are but a few of the questions we asked as we read through the papers contained in Justice Blackmun's and Powell's collections.

Importantly, our aim was not to be systematic in terms of quantifying the prevalence of one objective or tactic versus another, but rather to begin to identify the character of dissent coalition bargaining and negotiation. We recognize the limitations inherent in using select judicial papers. First, there may not be a physical record of in-person or telephone communications among the justices, let alone their clerks who act as informal ambassadors in the clerk network by routinely discussing cases across chambers. According to Murphy (1964): "Collections of letters and memoranda are always incomplete records; this is especially true of papers of men who are in daily face-to-face contact with each other or who frequently use the telephone" (ix).

Second, not every justice negotiates in every case. It is not uncommon for two justices to communicate privately and exclude the other members of the coalition or the Court as a whole. This was the case in *Cory v. White* (1982), where Justices Brennan and Powell bargained privately by memo over Justice Powell's principal dissent.[1] Neither Justices Marshall nor John Paul Stevens were included in the exchange even though both were in the dissent coalition. There would be no evidence of this bargaining in the papers of any of the justices except Justices Brennan and Powell; there is also the possibility that Justices Marshall and Stevens engaged in their own private discussions, but this evidence would similarly not appear in the papers of Justices Powell and Brennan. Thus, our goal was to identify *how* the process of dissent coalition formation and bargaining takes place, rather than *how often*.

Further, our goal was to explore how the legal and policy dialogue that takes place on the Court—and eventually shapes the formation of law and policy in the United States—manifests itself during the dissent coalition-formation process. As we show in the next chapter, the majority will, not uncommonly, discuss the dissent in its opinion. We argue that a fundamental building block to understanding why the majority will add the dissent into the formal, ongoing, public debate is dependent upon understanding the bargaining and accommodation that occurs between potential dissenters that shapes who dissents, why, and the ultimate content of the dissenting opinion. We use the justices' papers to identify both a major goal of the dissent negotiations—strengthening the dissent and attempting to become the majority—as well as the various ways these negotiations manifest.

NOT AT REST: CHIPPING AWAY AT THE MAJORITY

The dissent coalition comprises those justices who were in the minority of a split Conference vote, and any additional justices they can persuade to join their side during the opinion-writing process. A central component of dissent coalition formation is thus the attempt by minority justices to persuade their fellow justices to defect from the majority and join them. And defections are not uncommon. For example, in *North Haven Board of Education v. Bell* (1982), Chief Justice Warren Burger and Justice Powell were in dissent, and Justice Powell circulated his principal dissent to the Conference. Justice Powell wrote Chief Justice Burger: "Bill Rehnquist voted with the majority at Conference, but he was persuaded by my dissent, and has joined it."[2] Similarly, in *Williams v. Commissioner of Internal Revenue* (1977), Justice Potter Stewart was the sole dissenter at Conference. After Justice Stewart circulated his dissent, Justice Powell was persuaded to join him.[3]

While in the vast majority of cases justices' Conference votes are fairly settled, in some cases, justices use the opinion-writing process to definitively choose their preferred side. Opportunities to take votes from the majority coalition are therefore particularly acute when majority coalition justices explicitly indicate that they are "not at rest," meaning that their Conference votes were tentative. In *Arkansas Louisiana Gas Co. v. Hall* (1981), after Chief Justice Burger assigned the majority opinion to Justice Marshall and Justice Stevens was assigned the principal dissent, Justice Powell wrote the chief: "As indicated at Conference, I was not at rest in this confusing case. . . . I would like to be persuaded by what John intends to write. Accordingly, I will await what he writes, hoping to be able to affirm."[4] As is customary, Justice Powell copied all the justices on the memo so that Justice Stevens knew that Justice Powell's vote could be had. But Justice Stevens was not successful in persuading Justice Powell to join his opinion. Ultimately, Justice Powell issued his own dissent after reading Justice Stevens's principal dissent.

In *Aldinger v. Howard* (1976), Justice Blackmun's clerk David Patterson reviewed then-Associate Justice William Rehnquist's proposed majority opinion and wrote his boss: "I think the opinion is joinable. . . . I would wait to see the dissent, however. The sustained criticism that Justice Brennan is likely to give might point up some dangers that we have not seen, leading us to concur only in the judgment or in part of the opinion."[5] Following Justice Rehnquist's second circulation, Patterson wrote to Justice Blackmun: "I have sketched out a special concurrence that I think would allow you to join the result. . . . I note that your vote at Conference was tentative, however, and that should give you reason to wait for the dissent. I would prefer to do so."[6] After reviewing Justice Brennan's dissent, Patterson again wrote his boss: "Following your expression of interest in joining Justice Rehnquist's contrary opinion if possible, I suggested a way to reconcile doing so. . . . I urged you to await [Brennan's] dissent, however, suspecting that it might blow this theory out of the water. I think it has done so. . . . I would join the dissent."[7] Ultimately, Justice Brennan's dissent caused Justice Blackmun to defect to the minority.

Sometimes members of the majority coalition fail to quickly join a circulated majority opinion and instead indicate that they will await the dissent before making their final decision. For example, after Justice Marshall circulated his majority opinion in *Patsy v. Board of Regents* (1982), Justice Rehnquist wrote him: "Although I voted for the result which your opinion reaches at Conference, I have some difficulty with your treatment of the Eleventh Amendment issues in the opinion, and will await any separate writing that may be forthcoming. As a last resort, I may write separately myself."[8] Chief Justice Burger and Justice Powell had dissented at Conference, and Justice Powell immediately responded to Justice Marshall: "In due course, I will circulate a dissent."[9] Justice Sandra Day O'Connor echoed Justice Rehnquist: "I will await the additional writing in this case before finally deciding whether to join the Court's opinion."[10] Justice Byron White wrote: "Although I voted to reverse, I shall await the dissent. In any event, I may well write [separately]."[11] In the end, Justice Powell was not able to gain any defections and barely held Chief Justice Burger's vote. Justice Powell wrote his clerk: "Disappointing—but perhaps helpful long term."[12]

Another example of justices indicating they are waiting for the dissent before deciding whether or not to join the majority opinion is the case of *City of Eastlake v. Forest City Enterprises* (1976). Following Chief Justice Burger's majority opinion circulation, Justice Powell wrote him: "Your excellent opinion reflects the vote of the Conference, including my own vote, and I may very well join you. I do have second thoughts, however. . . . I will, therefore, await John Stevens' dissent hoping that he can identify a rationale that supports my basic instinct that we are about to step off the edge of a cliff."[13] He wrote the chief: "Although I still have doubts about the case and want to study it more closely before I finally decided which way to go, I presently believe that I will prepare a dissent in due course."[14] Ultimately, Justice Powell defected from the majority but issued his own dissent rather than join Justice Stevens's principal dissent.

Majority coalition members may go further than simply indicating that they are awaiting the dissent. They may also bargain with the author of the principal dissent. Following Justice White's circulation of his draft opinion in *Cory v. White* (1982), Justice Powell's clerk Dick Fallon wrote his justice: "I recommend that you indicate an intention to dissent in due course. . . . BRW's [Byron R. White's opinion] may not be equally acceptable to all members of the Conference majority. . . . [H]e reads [the precedents] much more narrowly than WJB [William J. Brennan] and TM [Thurgood Marshall] presumably would like to do. . . . I therefore would not be surprised if this opinion took some time to win the necessary votes. Its final form might influence the appropriate content of a dissent."[15] Justice Powell circulated a dissent, Justice Stevens joined, and Justice Brennan sent a bargaining memo to Justice Powell: "I am still pretty much at sea in these cases. I voted with Byron [White] but I must say your dissent gives me pause. I do think I am more with you than with him . . . [but] I am troubled about taking so large a step. In any event, where would you stop your approach . . . ?"[16] Justice Powell responded: "Your insightful questions have moved me to make two changes on the last page of my draft opinion. . . . I appreciate your sharing your thoughts with me. I would be happy to discuss any further ideas that you might have concerning this troublesome case."[17] Justice Powell gained Justice Marshall's vote but no one else's. Justice Brennan wrote Justice Powell: "I gather from the votes of the last day or two that you are not going to be able to get a Court in the above on your opinion. While I thought that was possible, I had hoped you and I could arrive at some accommodation. . . . I think I'll just circulate a concurrence."[18]

A second example of a majority coalition member bargaining with the principal dissent took place in *Pembaur v. City of Cincinnati* (1986). After Justice Powell circulated his principal dissent, Justice O'Connor wrote him with questions about the arguments in his draft. Justice Powell responded to her queries and concluded: "I appreciate your giving me the opportunity to address your concern, and hope that you will agree with Part I of my dissent. I also would rejoice if you also joined Part II."[19] Ultimately, Justice O'Connor did not defect to the dissenters. However, rather than join the majority opinion she issued her own opinion concurring in part and concurring the judgment. She explained to Justice Powell: "I should have written you before circulating my opinion concurring in the judgment in this case. I have very mixed feelings about the case and I finally decided, reluctantly, to adhere to my original conference vote."[20]

In some instances, gaining votes from the majority coalition may successfully turn the minority into the majority. For example, in *California v. Rooney* (1987), Justice Stevens's dissent caused both Justices Antonin Scalia and O'Connor to defect from the majority and give Justice Stevens five votes for his position. Justice Scalia wrote the Conference: "I have reviewed the record in this case and reluctantly conclude that the new point John raises in his dissent is correct, and we are without jurisdiction. . . . I change my vote to D.I.G."[21] Justice O'Connor wrote: "I have reluctantly concluded we should dismiss this case as improvidently granted and I would now vote to do so."[22]

Similarly, in *Buffalo Forge Co. v. United Steelworkers* (1976), Chief Justice Burger assigned the 5–4 majority opinion to Justice Stevens. Justice Stevens's circulation was followed three days later by Justice White's dissent. Justice White made one revision and recirculated his dissent two days later. Two days after that, Chief Justice Burger wrote Justice White: "I must say that I like John [Steven]'s result better than yours and that's the way Congress ought to provide. However, Congress did not, and I therefore join you."[23] Justice Stevens redrafted his majority opinion as the principal dissent, recirculated it, and it was joined by the other members of the former majority minus Chief Justice Burger.

In other cases, justices may strategically act during the coalition-formation process to try to achieve this ultimate win: in *Texaco v. Short* (1982), Justice Brennan circulated his dissent to the four justices in the minority coalition—one of whom was Justice Powell. Justice Powell's clerk John Wiley sensed an opportunity to gain a fifth vote and steal the majority if his justice acted fast: "I think this is an excellent dissent. If HAB [Harry A. Blackmun] is persuaded it may even become an excellent majority opinion! I urge that you join."[24] In the end, Justice Blackmun did not defect to the dissenters despite Justice Powell's quick join on Justice Brennan's dissent.

In *Enmund v. Florida* (1982), Justice O'Connor was assigned to write the majority opinion, but was unable to hold the five-vote coalition together. Justice Powell wrote her: "It now appears that your fine opinion will not command a Court. . . . I do have one suggestion for your consideration. One of the weakest points in Byron [White]'s opinion is that it will result in a federal, constitutional law of 'intent.' You mention this at page 24 of your opinion. It may be worth emphasizing."[25] Justice O'Connor replied: "I am somewhat frustrated and quite concerned that my draft failed to attract a majority. . . . I will incorporate your concerns in what will now become a dissent. In this business one must learn to 'grin and bear it.'"[26] After Justice O'Connor circulated her redrafted opinion—now a dissent—Justice Powell informed his staff: "Not a strong reply to BRW's Court opinion but I'll join"[27]

Justices who vote with the majority in Conference but place considerable constraints on the coalition may also ultimately defect to the minority if they are dissatisfied with the majority opinion. For example, in *Foremost Insurance Co. v. Richardson* (1982), Chief Justice Burger wrote Justice Powell: "At conference I voted to affirm if it were done 'narrowly.' Thurgood [Marshall] has tried to do it 'narrowly' but I now conclude the disposition just can't be so quantified. I therefore join your dissent."[28]

There is some evidence that justices seek to bolster minority coalitions by picking up votes from the majority coalition even if the minority will continue to remain the minority. Consider *Commonwealth Edison v. Montana* (1981). There were only three dissenting votes at Conference: Justices Blackmun, Powell, and Stevens. Justice Blackmun undertook the dissent, and Justice Powell wrote him both with suggestions about what to write and how to gain a fourth vote: "As you will recall, at Conference Byron [White] said that he could be 'had' to our point of view in this case."[29] In the end, Justice White did not defect and instead issued a concurring opinion in the case.

There may also be an attempt by a justice in the minority coalition to come up with a compromise solution that everyone might be able to agree with. Justice Powell undertook this course in *Patterson v. New York* (1977). He first sent his colleagues a memorandum written by one of his clerks—Dave Martin— attempting to find consensus by exploring various options in the case. Justice Powell summarized the arguments in his cover letter and concluded: "The views expressed above do not necessarily reflect my final thinking about these cases. No entirely satisfactory resolution of the issues presented has yet occurred to me or been suggested by others. I remain open to more attractive solutions."[30] Later in the day he sent his colleagues an advance copy of a law review article from two former clerks and laid out their arguments. He concluded: "In any event, and with no great enthusiasm, I share with you the views."[31] Unable to reach consensus, Justice White circulated a majority opinion and Justice Powell issued a dissent in which Justices Brennan and Marshall joined.

"SHAKING THE CASE"

As the above examples suggest, another crucial component of dissent coalition formation, one which is somewhat distinct from those driving majority coalition considerations, is timing. Should the principal dissent circulate before or after the majority opinion? Circulating the dissent first might persuade majority coalition members to defect. For example, in *County of Washington, Oregon v. Gunther* (1981), Chief Justice Burger was in the four-justice dissent coalition. He wrote Justice Stewart: "Are you willing to take on a dissent in this case? You recall Byron [White] said his vote to affirm was 'tentative.' A swift dissent might 'shake' the case."[32] Justice Stewart replied: "Rather than preparing a 'swift' dissent I would prefer to wait to see what the Court is going to say, and may well end up by joining the Court opinion."[33] Undeterred, Chief Justice Burger turned to Justice Rehnquist: "Since Potter [Stewart] 'opts out of the class,' will you put your hand to it?"[34] Justice Rehnquist accepted, but his draft did not circulate until six days after the majority circulation; he held Justice Stewart's vote, but was unable to persuade Justice White to defect.

Similarly, in *Pembaur v. City of Cincinnati* (1986), Justice Powell waited to circulate his dissent until after the majority opinion circulated, a decision that ultimately cost him a vote. He wrote his law clerk: "Justice Marshall who voted with us initially, changed his mind and has joined Justice Brennan's opinion."[35] Justice Powell himself nearly switched from the minority to the majority in *Arizona v. Hicks* (1987) when Justice Scalia's majority opinion circulated before Justice O'Connor's principal dissent. Justice Powell wrote Justice Scalia: "In view of our telephone conversation I have taken a close look at your carefully written opinion. It is as narrowly written as it could be and still affirm. With reluctance, I nevertheless write to say that I cannot join you. . . . I write in this detail, Nino, because I do admire that narrowness of your opinion."[36] Justice Scalia replied: "I am grateful for your taking the pain to explain at such length why you cannot come along in the above case. I entirely understand. . . . Although we both end where we began, I have no regrets about trying to reach an accommodation, as I hope you do not as well."[37] In the end, Justice Powell both joined the principal dissent and issued his own separate dissenting opinion.

Alternatively, in *Burger v. Kemp* (1987), Justice Powell prepared a draft dissent before both the majority opinion and Justice Blackmun's principal dissent were circulated, but decided not to circulate his dissent until after Justice

Blackmun's was circulated two months later. He wrote his clerk: "I would like to be able to circulate our dissent promptly after the Court opinion is circulated. Of course, what is written in the opinion may require some changes. Also Harry was asked to write the dissent. . . . Perhaps we should await Justice Blackmun's dissent, unhappily."[38] Following the circulation of the majority opinion, Justice Powell wrote his clerk: "Since we will circulate after HAB (but promptly), perhaps we should start with a reference to his dissent: 'Justice Powell, dissenting. Although I agree with much of Justice Blackmun's dissent and with his conclusion, I would reverse the judgment of the Court of Appeals on [a different] ground.'"[39] Following Justice Blackmun's circulation, Justice Powell wrote him: "Please join me in Part II of your dissent, and in the holding. . . . As I stated at Conference, however, I would reverse the decision below on [a different] ground. . . . I therefore write separately to emphasize [this]."[40] In sum, even though Justice Powell's separate dissent was drafted well in advance of the principal dissent, he made no attempt to shake the other dissenters—Blackmun, Brennan, and Marshall—via a preemptive circulation. In the end, Justices Marshall and Brennan joined Justice Blackmun's dissent, but only Justice Brennan also joined Justice Powell's.

Just as a well-timed, early dissent may shake majority coalition members, it may also cause the other dissenters to forgo writing their own dissents. For example, in *Young v. United States ex. rel. Vuitton et Fils* (1987), Chief Justice Rehnquist planned to draft the principal dissent, and Justice White indicated that he would await its circulation. However, Justice Powell quickly circulated an opinion concurring and dissenting in part. Chief Justice Rehnquist wrote him: "Please join me in your dissent. I no longer plan to write anything myself."[41] Justice White neither bargained with nor joined Justice Powell's opinion and instead issued his own dissent. These timing discussions reveal some of the important strategic considerations that are central to the dissent coalition-formation process, and somewhat distinct from those driving majority coalition deliberations.

HERDING CATS: CORRALLING THE DISSENTERS

While the dissenting justices try hard to chip away at the majority, most dissenting coalitions do not transform into the final majority coalition. A main goal of the principal dissent author is therefore to secure joins from the other justices in the minority. Just as the majority opinion author is tasked to write an opinion that reflects the broad consensus of the majority coalition, the minority opinion author also seeks to reflect the views of the entire minority coalition. Dissenters similarly bargain and negotiate with each other both to keep the dissenting coalition together, and to also try to forestall the issuance of additional, separate dissents. According to Beverly Blair Cook, "the goal of the [dissent] assigner is to produce a single dissent. By articulating the arguments of the minority, the opinion gives a legitimacy to its point of view that discourages defection" (1995, 23).

In general, our review of the justices' papers reveals that dissent coalition bargaining over opinion content is quite similar to majority coalition negotiations. Perhaps most important, clerks and justices strategize to craft principal dissents in ways that will gain joins from the members of the minority coalition and quash potential separate dissents. A dissent with more joiners likely sends important signals about the strength of the dissent to both internal as well as external audiences. And, as we explicated in the introduction and will show in chapter 3, the majority is more likely to cite a dissent with a larger number of joiners, probably because it poses a larger threat to the majority's position than dissents joined by only one or two justices. Since each justice is free to pen her own dissent, principal dissent authors try to bargain with and accommodate their colleagues in order to present a united front. For example, in *Connecticut v. Teal* (1982), Justice Powell was assigned the principal dissent. His clerk Mary Becker drafted it and wrote him: "There appears to be some dispute . . . among the dissenters. I believe you would prefer the prima-facie-case approach, but Justice O'Connor indicated at Conference that she considered the bottom-line argument a defense to the prima facie case. By avoiding the issue in the dissent, perhaps we can avoid separate (additional) dissents."[42] Justice Powell responded: "As you noted in your memo to me, the dissenters expressed varying reasons. Justice O'Connor, according to my notes, dissented tentatively on the 'burden of proof' approach. . . . I think this is the reasoning that [Powell clerk] Dick [Fallon] also preferred. Talk to Dick about the possibility of adding, as an alternative basis for the dissent, a paragraph or two that makes this argument."[43] Ultimately, Justice Powell's dissent was the only one issued with joins from Justice O'Connor and the others who dissented at Conference.

In a perfect world, the principal dissent author will issue a single dissenting opinion signed onto by the entirety of the minority coalition without any further bargaining or negotiation. Such "unconditional joins" result in a single, unified dissenting opinion being issued. Unconditional joins may occur even when the principal dissent is problematic to a minority coalition member to one extent or another. For example, in *Lawrence Cantor, dba Selden Drugs Co. v. The Detroit Edison Co.* (1976), Justice Stewart circulated the principal dissent on which Justice Powell noted: "This is unnecessarily long, discursive + not well organized. Also tone is a bit polemic. But decision is plainly right. Join."[44] Similarly, in *Transcontinental Gas Pipe Line Co. v. State Oil and Gas Board of Mississippi* (1986), Justice Rehnquist circulated a dissent and Justice Powell told his clerk: "Although I may have written some of this differently, (more strongly!) I'll join (I requested to draft a dissent for those of us sharing my view)."[45]

Numerous instances exist where justices join the dissent, but also provide suggestions with the hopes the opinion author will adopt them. *Bullington v. Missouri* (1981) is an example of this phenomenon. There were four dissenting votes in Conference: Chief Justice Burger and Justices White, Powell, and Rehnquist. Justice Powell was assigned the dissent and circulated his first draft. Justice Rehnquist joined but asked for a minor change: "On page 7 of your first . . . draft . . . footnote 3 states. . . . I would appreciate it if you could see your way clear to add, after that statement, a citation. . . . However, my preference is only that, and I do not condition my 'join' of your dissenting opinion on your making the change."[46] Justice Powell made the change. Chief Burger wrote Justice Powell: "I have already joined your dissent—but see 'thoughts while shaving' on attached pages."[47] Chief Justice Burger enclosed the pages of Justice Powell's draft with both his and his clerk's handwritten comments. Justice Powell's clerk Greg Morgan wrote his justice: "I have considered the Chief Justice's editing suggestions. I strongly recommend that we not accept any of his suggestions for 'improving' the middle paragraph on page 4. These suggestions would blur or even change our meaning. I see no harm in accepting the remaining three changes he suggests."[48] Justice Powell replied to Morgan: "I talked to C.J. + advanced that I would make some changes, but this would require recirculation, + postpone announcing decision."[49] In the end, Justice Powell's dissent garnered three joins and was the only dissent issued.

When principal dissents fail to secure unconditional joins from the outset, dissenting justices may bargain over their content. We identify four distinct variations of dissent coalition bargaining and negotiation. These deliberations are an important component of the broader law and policy dialogue, and the ultimate outcome may again have important implications for whether, as we explore more in chapter 3, the majority highlights and responds to the dissent in its own opinion.

The Conditional Join

If the principal dissent does not satisfy the members of the minority coalition, bargaining between the dissenters may transpire, just as it does between members of the majority. The most common form of dissent coalition bargaining, similar to what we see with majority coalition negotiations (see, e.g., Maltzman, Spriggs, and Wahlbeck 2000), occurs after the principal dissent is circulated when minority coalition members might condition their joins on changes to the dissenting opinion. The goal of this bargaining is, in the view of the justice asking for changes, to strengthen the principal dissent and ensure it reflects her views; the goal from the perspective of the principal dissent author is to try to stave off separate dissents from emerging.

An example is *Monroe v. Standard Oil Co.* (1981) where Justice Powell voted with the minority at Conference. But, after Justice Stewart's majority opinion circulated, Justice Powell informed his clerk: "I was in dissent at Conference. This is a strong opinion. I'll review the case before deciding what to do. I'll await the dissent."[50] When Chief Justice Burger circulated his dissent, Justice Powell's clerk Paul Smith wrote: "You voted to dissent. This is a fair statement of the dissenting position in a case where neither view is very attractive. By the way, PS [Potter Stewart]'s Court opinion only has 3 joins so far. P.S. The CJ said this version was only tentative. You probably should wait at least until the next circulation."[51] Justice Powell replied to his clerks: "I agree with Paul Smith that neither side of this case is attractive. I believe, however, I'll stay with my vote to reverse."[52] Chief Justice Burger then revised his introductory paragraph and recirculated his dissent. Justice Powell's clerk Smith took issue with the final sentence and wrote Justice Powell: "This new sentence seems out of place, especially since the dissent fails to show why it is true. Moreover, such a consideration is irrelevant to this question of statutory construction."[53] Justice Powell agreed and asked Chief Justice Burger to "omit the last sentence," enclosed a newspaper story supporting his "very strongly held view," and explained that he did "not wish to associate my name" with the statement.[54] The chief deleted the sentence, and Justice Powell joined his opinion. While such a change may appear small on its face, Justice Powell's vote gave Chief Justice Burger's dissent four votes instead of three, kept Justice Powell from writing separately, and prevented him from possibly defecting to the majority.

Another example of bargaining by potential joiners occurred in *Lee v. Illinois* (1986). Justice Powell replied to Justice Blackmun's principal dissent circulation: "Although I think the substance of your dissent is excellent, there

are three sentences that appear to be inconsistent with our recent decision. . . .
As you know, Bill Brennan's opinion in *Lee* expressly does not deal with the
issue of unavailability. Therefore, it is not necessary in dissent to address the
issue of unavailability at all."[55] Justice Blackmun replied: "I am endeavoring
to accommodate your concerns."[56] On receipt of Justice Blackmun's revised
dissent, Justice Powell wrote his clerk: "Harry has made minimal changes in
response to my letter. . . . I think I can accept his changes."[57]

Sometimes these negotiations are not successful, especially if multiple
members of the dissenting coalition differ on certain points or justices feel it
necessary to highlight particular, or additional, arguments. *Goodman v. Lukens
Steel Co.* (1987) offers a clear example of the difficulties of accommodating
multiple justices' concerns: Justice O'Connor initially joined Justice Powell's
principal dissent, but Justice Powell revised its content when Justice Scalia
indicated his join was conditional. Justice Scalia wrote Justice Powell: "If you
can see your way clear to dropping footnote 1, I will join the opinion in its
entirety; otherwise, please show me as not joining the footnote in whatever
manner seems appropriate."[58] After Justice Powell dropped the footnote, Justice O'Connor wrote him: "I notice in your most recent circulation . . . you
have omitted n. 1. . . . I assume this was done in response to Nino's letter to
you. . . . My own view is captured in your former footnote and I am reluctant
to see it dropped. Is there a possibility you might restore it or would you prefer
I write something separately?"[59] Justice Powell replied: "I owe you an apology,
as I certainly should have talked to you before I omitted n. 1 in my opinion. . . .
As you suggest, I did this in response to Nino's letter. . . . In the circumstances,
I suppose it is best to leave my opinion as circulated . . . without the footnote."[60] Justice O'Connor responded by joining Justice Powell's opinion in
part and also issuing her own dissent.

Similarly, in *Mississippi University for Women v. Hogan* (1982), Chief Justice
Burger wrote Justice Powell: "I agree with your dissent in this case. However,
I am concerned about your characterization of the Court's opinion. . . . Over-
stating the scope of the Court's holding can create problems. I fear such statements may come back to haunt us. I can heartily join a narrower approach"[61]
Justice Powell replied, defending his characterization of Justice O'Connor's
majority opinion: "If Sandra, in a response to my dissent, argues [the point
you raise] . . . I will then address her argument. For it to be at all persuasive,
however, she would have to revise a great deal of the rhetoric, as well the holding, in her opinion."[62] Justice Powell did not make the change Chief Justice

Burger suggested, and the chief decided to issue his own dissent rather than join Justice Powell's principal dissent.

Members of the minority coalition may not be able to join a principal dissent unreservedly but will still bargain over various parts in order to join as much as possible. Consider *Martin v. Ohio* (1987). Following Justice Powell's circulation of the principal dissent, Justice Blackmun wrote him: "I . . . cannot join Part II of your dissent. I can join Part III, however, and would join Part I if the third sentence and the first word of the fourth sentence were omitted or if some other accommodation were made. If you could modify that small segment of Part I, I would then join all of your opinion except Part III. This is my preference."[63] Justice Powell agreed, and Justice Blackmun joined all but Part III. Justice Rehnquist proposed a similar change to Justice Stevens's principal dissent in *Doyle v. Ohio* (1976). Justice Stevens replied: "I cannot totally accept your suggestion. However, I wonder if the attached revision would make it possible for you to join Part II B?"[64] Justice Rehnquist agreed to the changes and ultimately joined all of Justice Stevens's dissent.

Wooley v. Maynard (1977) offers another example of this phenomenon. After Justice White circulated his opinion concurring and dissenting in part, Justice Rehnquist wrote him: "Please join me in your separate opinion. . . . I am also preparing a separate dissent on the merits."[65] Justice Blackmun similarly wrote Justice White: "You have described your circulation as one 'concurring in part and dissenting in part.' I am not concurring in the Court's opinion, so if you could change your description to 'dissenting in part,' I could join you and hereby do."[66] On seeing Justice Blackmun's memo, Justice Rehnquist wrote Justice White: "I think Harry's letter to you . . . is probably a sounder analysis of our relationship, as dissenters on the merits, to your partial dissent, than was my simple 'join' letter to you earlier. It would please me, too, therefore, if you could make the change which Harry suggests."[67] Justice White agreed. Justice Rehnquist still issued his separate dissent, which Justice Blackmun also joined.

Bargaining Initiated by the Principal Dissenter

Bargaining can also be initiated by the principal dissenter. In these instances, the principal dissenter may send a bargaining memo in conjunction with the principal dissent. For example, in *Singleton v. Wulff* (1976), Justice Powell circulated his principal dissent to the three other justices in minority coalition with the following note: "One or two of the footnotes express views that are unnecessary to the decision, and that reflect my own thinking. These can be modified or omitted if one or more of you should otherwise be disposed to join my opinion."[68] Ultimately, the others joined and did not issue separate opinions.

Principal dissenters may also initiate bargaining if other dissents are circulated. For example, Justice Powell circulated the principal dissent in *California Coastal Commission v. Granite Rock Co.* (1987), and Justice Scalia circulated a separate dissent. Justice Powell's clerk Ronald Mann wrote his boss: "I recommend that you not join Justice Scalia's opinion. . . . I recommend that you take no action. I note that there is little in Justice Scalia's opinion that would preclude him from joining your dissent. I am disappointed that he did not consider doing so."[69] Justice Powell wrote Justice Scalia: "I have now had an opportunity to take a look at your dissent. . . . I do not think your opinion is necessarily inconsistent with my dissenting opinion. If there are changes I could make that would enable you to join my dissent, I would be glad to consider them."[70] Justice Scalia responded, "Much as I would like to merge our dissents, I am afraid that I do not agree with the fundamental proposition [you make]. . . . I cannot imagine any suggested revision of your opinion that would overcome that difficulty. Would it be possible for you to reconsider the question [raised by] . . . my opinion? . . . . Whether we can get together or not, I appreciate your effort at trying. I will be happy to talk the matter over if you think that would be useful."[71] In the end, the positions were irreconcilable, and each justice issued his own dissent without joining the other.

Preemptive Bargaining
A less common form of dissent bargaining occurs *prior* to circulation of the principal dissent, what we term "preemptive bargaining." Preemptive bargaining is a subtle form of negotiation that takes place among dissent coalition members soon after the initial Conference vote. Preemptive bargaining can take two forms. First, it can occur at the dissent assignment stage. For example, in *Ridgway v. Ridgway* (1981), Justice Powell wrote Justice Stevens: "As you, Bill Rehnquist and I are in dissent in this case, I will try my hand on the fraud theory that I mentioned at Conference. If I understand the theory you mentioned, I am afraid it will be difficult to reconcile with our decisions. But, if you write, you may possibly persuade me."[72] Justice Stevens responded: "I will make an effort to persuade you that our prior decisions do not control this case. I think Tom Clark left the door wide open in his *Wissner* opinion."[73] Following Justice Powell's principal dissent circulation, Justice Stevens circu-

lated his own dissent but was unable to persuade Justice Powell to budge. In the end, only Justice Rehnquist joined Justice Powell's principal dissent, and Justice Stevens issued his dissent without any joins.

Similarly, in *Steadman v. SEC* (1981), Justices Stewart and Powell were in dissent at Conference. Justice Stewart wrote Justice Powell: "I suggest that we ask Bill Brennan to append the following at the foot of his opinion for the Court in this case: Justice Stewart and Justice Powell dissent. They believe . . ."[74] Justice Stewart's two-sentence dissenting note led to considerable discussion among the two justices and their clerks about the substance of the dissent. Justice Powell's clerk Paul Cane wrote his justice: "I am reluctant to interfere with Justice Stewart's expeditious method of handling the dissent in this case. Nevertheless, my re-reading of [the precedents] suggests to me that his proposal does not do justice to the best line of reasoning that can be marshaled for the dissenting view."[75] Justice Powell phoned Justice Stewart and ultimately the two decided that Justice Powell's clerk should draft a brief dissenting opinion. Justice Powell wrote Cane: "I have talked to P.S. + he suggests we simply rely on the CADC cases."[76] Cane replied: "You wondered whether it would be possible to write a two- or three-page dissent in this case sketching out our grounds for disagreement with the majority. I quickly drafted a short one, and it is attached. It is obviously rough, but I give it to you in this form now so that you can decide whether it's worth pursuing."[77] Justice Powell sent it to Justice Stewart: "Here is the short dissent that I mentioned yesterday. I have preference for something along these lines."[78] Justice Stewart ultimately withdrew his original dissenting note and joined Justice Powell's dissent.

The second way that preemptive bargaining takes place is when a member of the minority coalition issues a preemptive memorandum to attempt to influence the principal dissent. This form of preemptive bargaining occurred in *Nyquist v. Mauclet* (1977). After Justice Blackmun circulated a majority opinion, Justice Rehnquist informed the Conference that he would circulate a dissent in due course, and Chief Justice Burger—who had assigned the principal dissent to Rehnquist—wrote his colleagues: "I am giving thought to circulating a dissent along the lines of the attached typed draft. Alternatively, I will likely join Bill's dissent."[79] We suggest that Chief Justice Burger's circulated dissent—in advance of Justice Rehnquist's—is a form of preemptive bargaining. Ultimately, Chief Justice Burger both issued his dissent and joined Justice Rehnquist's. He also joined another separate dissent by Justice Powell, which Justice Stewart also joined. There is no evidence in the Powell Papers of bargaining beyond the chief's initial memo.

Unwillingness to Bargain

Finally, sometimes members of the dissent coalition are simply unwilling to bargain, determining that writing separately—and potentially decreasing the strength of the principal dissent—is necessary. Given that the majority opinion is, by definition, a reflection of the majority justices' collective decision, this lack of bargaining is distinct to dissenting blocs. For example, in *Bender v. Williamsport Area School District* (1986), Chief Justice Burger circulated the principal dissent, but Justice Powell neither joined nor attempted to bargain. Justice Powell noted at the top of Chief Justice Burger's draft: "I am not sure Douglas' opinion in *Zorach* is relevant. I might write separately + say that I agree there is standing + that *Widmar* controls."[80] Justice Powell similarly hedged in *International Union v. Brock* (1986) after reading Justice White's principal dissent: "I . . . am inclined to join BRW, or to write myself."[81] In the end, Justice Powell neither joined Justice White's dissent, nor attempted to bargain with him, and instead issued his own dissent.

Justices may also eschew bargaining because they do not anticipate that the principal dissenter will be amenable to their ideas. In *Charles D. Bonanno Linen Service, Inc. v. NLRB* (1982), Justice O'Connor informed Chief Justice Burger: "I plan to try writing a brief separate dissent . . . which would indicate my preference for a [new] rule. . . . I am uncomfortable with the 'all or nothing' approaches of both the majority and your proposed dissent."[82] Interestingly, she only sent her draft to Justice Powell and asked for his feedback. He made several suggestions and noted: "If you can accommodate them generally, I will be happy to join your dissent."[83] She agreed, and Justice Powell joined her, while Chief Justice Burger issued the principal dissent with Justice Rehnquist joining.

In other instances, justices may be uninterested in bargaining even if they are willing to join the principal dissent. For example, in *Clayton v. Automobile Workers* (1981), Chief Justice Burger and Justices Stewart, Rehnquist, and Powell were in dissent. The chief assigned the principal dissenting opinion to Justice Rehnquist, who circulated his draft after Justice Brennan's majority opinion was circulated. Justice Powell's clerk Greg Morgan reviewed the opinions and wrote Justice Powell: "I do not think that this is a strong dissent. Particularly, I do not find the response to Justice Brennan's 'second prong' (as the dissent calls it) very persuasive. Nor is it backed by much authority. You might await Justice Brennan's rejoinder, if any. But I am now inclined to recommend joining Justice Brennan, who has a Court."[84] Justice Powell considered Morgan's recommendation but did not defect to the majority. He also made no attempt to bargain with Justice Rehnquist. Rather, Justice Powell joined Justice Rehnquist's dissent unconditionally while also writing separately. He wrote Morgan: "I've written a separate opinion + joined WHR."[85]

An unwillingness to bargain appears to arise most frequently when justices wish to write separately to emphasize a specific point or to add an additional argument to the public record. For example, after Chief Justice Burger circulated his principal dissent in *Jacksonville Bulk Terminals v. Longshoremen* (1982), Justice Powell circulated a separate, brief dissent. Chief Justice Burger read it, incorporated Justice Powell's arguments, and recirculated. Justice Powell wrote his clerk: "I have now read the Chief's revised dissent in which he has added a new Part II. As you say, he largely plagiarizes my little opinion. I am still inclined, however, to stay with it."[86] Justice Powell joined the chief's dissent, but still wrote separately. He did the same thing in *Arizona v. Hicks* (1987), writing Justice O'Connor: "Please join me in your fine dissenting opinion. I may add a brief dissent for emphasis."[87] Justice Stevens acted similarly in *Colorado River Water Conservation District v. United States* (1976), writing the following note to principal dissent author Justice Stewart: "If I may, I would like to join your dissenting opinion while adding the additional comments reflected in the attached dissent."[88] In all of these instances, the justices did not attempt to bargain with the principal dissent author, with Justice Powell even going so far as to be somewhat indifferent to Chief Justice Burger's attempts to revise the principal dissent to reflect his arguments in *Jacksonville Bulk Terminals.*

Discussion and Conclusion

Understanding the effect a dissent may have on the national legal and policy dialogue, as well as on the justices' internal dialogue, necessitates understanding the role of dissents and dissent coalitions more broadly. The preceding chapter provides an overview of the major institutional developments on the Court that have enabled dissents to flourish. Each of these developments— from justices publicly acknowledging that they authored an opinion for the Court to the reduction of the Court's mandatory docket to the formalization of dissent assignments and bargaining—further entrenched a culture of dissent. And we propose that this entrenchment also helps illuminate the important role dissents play in the broader legal and policy debate. Chapter 1 also explores why and when justices are most likely to decide to vote to dissent in the modern era. We find that justices' decision-making is a function of legal, ideological, and strategic considerations, necessitating a comprehensive theory of judicial decision-making to fully understand the decision to dissent.

Once justices decide to dissent, the dissent coalition formation and bargaining process commences. While studies have examined in detail bargaining and negotiation between members of the majority coalition, no prior study has yet to examine bargaining and negotiation from the perspective of the dissenting justices. We offer in this chapter a first look at the content and variations in the communications between members of the dissenting coalition as well as potential dissenters. We argue that understanding this coalition formation process can also help shed light on when the majority will be most likely to feel it necessary to respond to a dissent in the majority opinion. The ultimate goal of dissenters is to craft the strongest possible principal dissent, and either shift from the minority to the majority, or at least stave off competing separate opinions; a stronger dissent can also be viewed as more worthy of response by the contemporaneous majority or of citation by a future majority.

The justices' papers reveal both straightforward editing suggestions as well as more intense negotiations centered around holding off both defections and additional dissenting opinions. We identify four variations of negotiations: conditional joins, bargaining initiated by the principal dissenter, preemptive bargaining prior to any drafts being circulated, and instances where justices eschew bargaining altogether. Some of these negotiations are successful, and others fail, but in almost all cases they reveal the justices' desire to work with their colleagues even as they strive to see their favored arguments enshrined in the formal record.

Refusals to bargain, alternatively, highlight how dissenting strategy differs in kind from that of the majority. Majority members must bargain to some degree, as they strive to craft a consensus document everyone can join. Dissents, on the other hand, inherently reflect when bargaining with one's colleagues has broken down, and so the papers suggest that some justices may decide that any additional bargaining—even with those also in dissent—is unnecessary. Dissenters thus must decide whether they even want to engage in a negotiation with other potential dissenters, or simply go it alone. And, as the cases we highlight above reveal, justices sometimes decide to chart a solo path, refusing to engage with their other dissenting colleagues.

This unwillingness to bargain and accommodate, however, may backfire on justices, even as they potentially achieve individual goals: as we show in the next chapter, dissents that more justices join are significantly more likely to be discussed by the contemporaneous majority than dissents with fewer signatories. Those findings therefore suggest that justices are well served by bargaining with their fellow dissenters, because presenting a unified position can aid their ability to have their views discussed in the majority opinion.

This investigation of the dissent coalition formation and bargaining process reveals the intricacies of the dissent-writing process. It also reveals that dissenters are cognizant of the necessity of ensuring their arguments are well explicated and heard, whether by other justices or outside actors. While dissenters may have lost in the present case, the ultimate goal is to convince one's colleagues—whether contemporaneous or future—to adopt the dissenters' arguments. One crucial step in that long-range plan is to ensure the dissent is included in the public, ongoing legal and policy dialogue by being cited by the majority. We explore this phenomenon, as well as what dissenting justices can potentially do to increase the likelihood of majority attention, in detail in the next chapter.

3 | Intra-Court Dialogue

Contemporaneous Effect of Dissents on Majority Opinions

ON SEPTEMBER 11, 1980, a young woman approached two police officers, Kraft and Scarring, who were on patrol in Queens, New York (*New York v. Quarles* 1984, 651). She told them that she had been raped, described the man to the officers, and then told them that the man was carrying a gun and had just gone into a nearby grocery store (651–52).

The officers drove to the grocery store. Officer Kraft entered the store to try to locate the suspect, while Office Scarring waited outside for backup. The man spotted Officer Kraft as he entered the store and ran toward the back. Officer Kraft caught up with him and ordered the man to stop. Upon reaching the suspect, Officer Kraft frisked him, discovering an empty shoulder holster. The officer then placed the man in handcuffs. At this point, Office Kraft asked the man where the gun was located; the man indicated some empty cartons, stating, "'the gun is over there'" (652). The officer subsequently located the gun, placed the man under arrest, and read him his *Miranda* rights. After the man indicated he would waive his right to wait for an attorney before answering any questions, Officer Kraft asked the man if the gun was his and, if so, where he purchased it. The man replied yes, and he had bought it in Miami, Florida.

The man, later identified as Benjamin Quarles, was prosecuted for criminal possession of a weapon. At trial, the judge did not allow either the statement, "'the gun is over there,'" or the gun itself to be introduced as evidence because Officer Kraft asked Quarles where the gun was located prior to *Mirandizing* him. The other statements about owning the gun and where he bought it were also excluded as stemming directly from the original *Miranda* violation. The appellate division of the Supreme Court of New York and the New York Court of Appeals both affirmed the trial court's decision.

In *New York v. Quarles* (1984), the United States Supreme Court reversed the lower courts, creating a "'public safety' exception to the requirement that *Miranda* warnings be given before a suspect's answers may be admitted into evidence" (655). Specifically, the exception applies when "police officers ask questions reasonably prompted by a concern for public safety," and "does not depend upon the motivation of the individual officers involved" (656).

According to the majority opinion,

> The police in this case, in the very act of apprehending a suspect, were confronted with the immediate necessity of ascertaining the whereabouts of a gun which they had every reason to believe the suspect had just removed from his empty holster and discarded in the supermarket. So long as the gun was concealed somewhere in the supermarket, with its actual whereabouts unknown, it obviously posed more than one danger to the public safety: an accomplice might make use of it, a customer or employee might later come upon it.

> In such a situation, if the police are required to recite the familiar *Miranda* warnings before asking the whereabouts of the gun, suspects in Quarles' position might well be deterred from responding. Procedural safeguards which deter a suspect from responding were deemed acceptable in *Miranda* in order to protect the Fifth Amendment privilege; when the primary social cost of those added protection is the possibility of fewer convictions, the *Miranda* majority was willing to bear that cost. Here, had *Miranda* warnings deterred Quarles from responding to Officer Kraft's question about the whereabouts of the gun, the cost would have been something more than merely the failure to obtain evidence useful in convicting Quarles. Officer Kraft needed an answer to his question not simply to make his case against Quarles but to insure that further danger to the public did not result from the concealment of the gun in a public area. (657)

Justice Thurgood Marshall dissented, joined by Justices William Brennan and John Paul Stevens. The dissent argued that "the majority has endorsed the introduction of coerced self-incriminating statements in criminal prosecutions" (674). According to the dissent:

> The "public-safety" exception departs from this principle by expressly inviting police officers to coerce defendants into making incriminating statements, and then permitting prosecutors to introduce those statements at trial. Though the majority's opinion is cloaked in the beguiling language of utilitarianism, the Court has sanctioned *sub silentio* criminal prosecutions based on compelled self-incriminating statements. I find

this result in direct conflict with the Fifth Amendment's dictate that "[n]o person . . . shall be compelled in any criminal case to be a witness against himself." (686)

The majority specifically responded in a footnote:

> The dissent curiously takes us to task for 'endors[ing] the introduction of coerced self-incriminating statements in criminal prosecutions,' *post,* at 674, and for 'sanction[ing] *sub silentio* criminal prosecutions based on compelled self-incriminating statements.' Of course our decision to-day does nothing of the kind. As the *Miranda* Court itself recognized, the failure to provide *Miranda* warnings in and of itself does not render a confession involuntary, and respondent is certainly free on remand to argue that his statement was coerced under traditional due process standards. Today we merely reject the only argument that respondent has raised to support the exclusion of his statement, that the statement must be *presumed* compelled because of Officer Kraft's failure to read him his *Miranda* warnings. (655) [citations omitted]

The dissent additionally argued:

> The irony of the majority's decision is that the public's safety can be perfectly well protected without abridging the Fifth Amendment. If a bomb is about to explode or the public is otherwise imminently imperiled, the police are free to interrogate suspects without advising them of their constitutional rights. Such unconsented questioning may take place not only when police officers act on instinct but also when higher faculties lead them to believe that advising a suspect of his constitutional rights might decrease the likelihood that the suspect would reveal life-saving information. If trickery is necessary to protect the public, then the po-lice may trick a suspect into confessing. While the Fourteenth Amend-ment sets limits on such behavior, nothing in the Fifth Amendment or our decision in *Miranda v. Arizona* proscribes this sort of emergency questioning. All the Fifth Amendment forbids is the introduction of coerced statements at trial. (686)

The majority again responded to the dissent's argument in a footnote:

The dissent argues that a public safety exception to *Miranda* is unnecessary because in every case an officer can simply ask the necessary questions to protect himself or the public, and then the prosecution can decline to introduce any incriminating responses at a subsequent trial. But absent actual coercion by the officer, there is no constitutional imperative requiring the exclusion of the evidence that results from police inquiry of this kind; and we do not believe that the doctrinal underpinnings of *Miranda* require us to exclude the evidence, thus penalizing officers for asking the very questions which are the most crucial to their efforts to protect themselves and the public. (658)

Why did the majority decide to respond to these arguments raised by the dissenters in *Quarles?* The majority could have simply ignored the dissenters' arguments, and did so in other cases that same term, such as *Pulley v. Harris* (1984) and *United States v. Jacobsen* (1984). What made them determine that the best course of action in *Quarles* was to address these opposing arguments directly, rather than not acknowledging them at all?

In this chapter, we examine the factors that explain which dissents have the biggest contemporaneous impact on the law—specifically, on the majority opinion that the dissent accompanies. The majority opinion writer must keep two main goals in mind: to accurately convey the reasoning of the majority coalition, and to do so in a way that keeps intact the majority coalition. In an ideal situation, the majority opinion author writes for a unanimous Court on a case where the legal answer is straightforward and clear, with no disagreements or even minor variations of opinions among the justices. In many cases, however, such as *Quarles,* some set of justices decide to dissent. We discussed in chapter 2 the process by which dissenting justices bargain and negotiate both among themselves as well as with the majority coalition to produce a dissenting opinion. In this chapter, we turn to the central question motivating this book: Why do some dissents, like Justice Marshall's dissent in *Quarles,* spur the majority to address them head-on?

Do We Respond or Do We Ignore?

The majority decision in each case before the Supreme Court reflects the Court's contribution to the broader legal and policy debate on a particular issue. According to Justice Anthony Kennedy, one of the main goals of the majority opinion author is to "convince the parties that you've understood their arguments. You must convince the attorneys that you've understood the law ... [and] [y]ou must command allegiance to your opinion" (Garner 2010, 84). The majority opinion will be read far and wide, from the parties to the case, to outside actors affected by the Court's rule and holding, such as interested legislators and executives, potential future litigants, lower court judges, lawyers, the media, and the broader public. Especially as the US Supreme Court increasingly hears fewer cases every year, more attention is directed to each of the relatively few decisions it hands down each term. As discussed more fully in the introduction, the Court's only mechanism to engage in the ongoing legal and policy dialogue is through its published opinions in cases. The decisions themselves are thus the sole record by which the Court communicates.

Sometimes, not all justices join the majority decision. Some justices may concur, agreeing with the outcome the majority reached but limiting, expanding, clarifying, or contradicting the majority opinion (see, e.g., Corley 2010). Other justices may dissent, disagreeing with the majority's decision in its entirety. We explicate in the introduction and chapter 1 why justices may dissent, and what goals they seek to achieve through these dissents. We further explore in chapter 2 the bargaining and negotiation process that occurs between the majority and dissenting justices as well as among the dissenting the justices themselves. Ultimately, it is only the majority opinion that reflects the decision of the Court, and it is only the majority opinion that serves as precedent.

When there is a dissent, the majority can decide to simply ignore the dissent, or it can address it directly. Ignoring the dissent deprives it of oxygen; however, by citing a dissent, and even possibly discussing it in depth, the Court shines a clear light on disagreeing voices. While a dissent will always be in the formal record of the votes of the Court, discussing a dissent in the majority opinion gives the dissenting views additional heft and attention. Citing a dissent also highlights for those outside the Court—whether lower court judges, other governmental actors, future litigants, members of the media, or the broader public—that they should be cognizant of the arguments offered by the dissenters. Between the 1953 and 2004 terms, 31.6 percent of dissents were cited by the corresponding majority opinion. Why did the majority in these cases choose to illuminate dissenting voices, thereby adding them formally into the dialogue? Under what circumstances does the majority decide a dissent is worthy of such attention? We explore these questions in this chapter.

In the beginning of the modern era, very few dissents were found by the Court to be worthy of such attention. Not only has the number of dissents themselves grown, but as shown in figure 10, so too has the proportion of majority/plurality opinions citing the accompanying dissent increased dramatically over time. It was not until the 1967 term that more than four dissents were mentioned by a majority opinion in a single term; the eleven dissents cited by the majority in 1967 still only accounted for 17 percent of all dissents that term. The 1981 term marked the first one where a higher proportion of dissents were cited by the majority opinion than not, with 57.5 percent of the accompanying dissents (61 out of 106) discussed by the majority. That term served as an outlier, however, until 1991. Since 1991, through where our data ends in 2004, dissents are more likely to be cited by the majority than not in every term but two (1993 and 1996).

Even as the percentage of dissents that are cited by the majority has grown, and even as the back-and-forth exchange between the justices in their opinions has become part of the public record, majority opinion writers continue to pick and choose which dissents they believe are worthy of discussion and which they ignore. Why are some cited and others not? As we explicate fully in the introduction, we argue the majority must determine whether it is more harmful to the majority to ignore the dissent or to directly address it. In cases where the majority decides the costs of not responding are higher than the benefits, the majority will discuss the dissent. What types of dissents are more

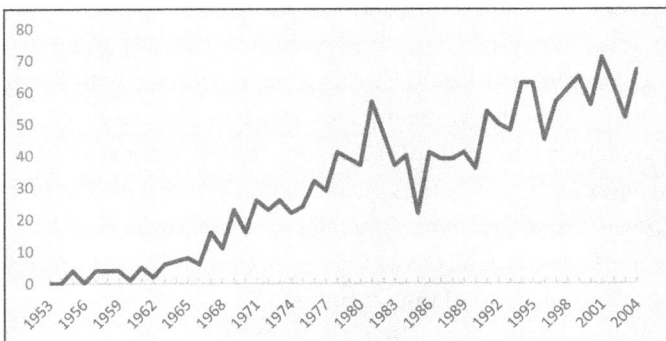

FIGURE 10. Proportion of majority/plurality opinions citing accompanying dissent, 1953–2004 terms

likely to be viewed by the majority as potentially harmful? We argue the most potentially harmful dissents are those that are well crafted, as well as those that have the highest likelihood of attracting external attention. In the next sections, we briefly summarize our theoretical framework while also detailing how we define and operationalize well-crafted and attention-grabbing dissents.

WELL-CRAFTED DISSENTS

We argue that judicial opinions, both majority opinions and dissents, are a form of persuasive writing, aimed at specific audiences. The purpose of a written judicial opinion is not for the judge to arrive at a conclusion since she has already done that. Instead, as Justice Kennedy explained, "the purpose of the opinion is to convince . . . based on what we write" (Garner 2010, 85). Through her opinion, the judge must present her conclusion along with the reasons for that conclusion, crafting a narrative that persuades specific audiences, such as the litigants, the attorneys representing them, other judges (including both colleagues and future judges), legislatures, the news media, and the public of its correctness (Stevenson 1975). And the most persuasive opinions are those that are well crafted. Producing a well-written and well-reasoned opinion is therefore a goal of all judges, whether they are writing a majority opinion or a dissent.

Given that "the most frequent objection to a dissent is that it weakens the force of the [majority] decision" (Urofsky 2017, 9), we posit that it is important for majority opinion authors to respond to arguments made by the dissent, especially if that dissent is well reasoned and well written. As explained in the introduction, Supreme Court justices have remarked on how important dissents are to the "intra-court dialogue" (Urofsky 2017, 11). Justice Ruth Bader Ginsburg argued that a dissenting opinion contributes to the improvement of the law, that "it heightens the [majority] opinion writer's incentive to 'get it right'" (Ginsburg 1990, 139). Justices thus recognize that a strong, well-written dissent poses a greater threat to the majority than one that is not.

We focus on three factors that all tap into different facets of strong writing. First, we examine the readability of the dissent. Mark Osbeck's (2012) seminal guide to legal writing states that "Clarity . . . is the most basic quality of good legal writing" (428). Judges should use simple language that the general reader can understand. "There is a place for the elegant word, but it should not be necessary for the reader to have a dictionary at hand while reading the opinion" (Federal Judicial Center 1991, 23). More complex opinions mean that fewer people can understand the judgment or reasoning of the court and raise the potential danger of the court losing its public voice (Vickrey, Denton, and Jefferson 2012).

Unclear opinions can undermine the substance of an argument because they risk confusion and misunderstanding on the part of the audience (M. R. Smith 2008). Chief Justice John Roberts has spoken about the importance of clear legal writing and his frustration when it is not clear: "[L]ack of clarity bothers me. If you just sit there and read a sentence and just have to go back and read it again . . . if [you're] slogging through each sentence because it's just not very clear . . . it becomes a real chore, as opposed to a pleasure" (Garner 2010, 11). Justice Clarence Thomas similarly admires "[s]implicity and clarity" in legal writing (Garner 2010, 99).

According to Justice Antonin Scalia:

> [T]he judge wants to make his opinion clear. And imprecision takes a terrible toll—especially if you're talking about appellate opinions—because the only important part about an appellate case is not who wins or loses; it's not, you know, affirmed or reversed. The important part is the opinion. And if you affirm or reverse for the wrong reason, you've done everything wrong. Especially at the Supreme Court, where we basically only take cases where there are disagreements on the law below, if you haven't made clear what your holding is, instead of reducing litigation, instead of making life simpler for courts and lawyers below you, you've complicated it. So it's very important that judges' opinions be clear. (Garner 2010, 54)

One month before his confirmation hearing, Judge Neil Gorsuch was profiled in a lengthy *Washington Post* article. The reporters noted: "Even the simple writing style of his opinions, which have won wide attention in legal circles, reflects his conviction that the law should be understandable to everyone, lest it favor only the wealthy and well educated. . . . Former clerks say that Gorsuch's insistence on clear writing reflects his convictions about making the law accessible and understandable to everyone" (Kindy, Horwitz, and Wan 2017).

There has long been a movement to use plain language in law and regulation and even business (Leonhardt 2000). The idea is to use the "simplest, most straightforward way of expressing an idea" (Garner 2001, xiv). "[T]he purpose of communication is to communicate, and this can't be done if the reader . . . doesn't understand the words used" (Garner 2013, 183). Justice Ginsburg advised: "If you can say it in plain English, you should" (Garner 2010, 141). According to Justice Stephen Breyer, he is against using legalese. "Legalese—you mean jargon? Legal jargon? Terrible! Terrible! I would try to avoid it as much as possible. No point. Adds nothing" (Garner 2010, 156). We argue that it is difficult for a legal opinion to achieve its core function, to persuade, if the reader has difficulty understanding it. A previous study finds that when given two otherwise identical passages seeking a rehearing of a particular matter, one written in "legalese" and the other in simpler English, participants judge the plainer style to be much more persuasive (Benson and Kessler 1987). Studies of lower court and agency compliance similarly find that compliance increases in response to more clearly written Court opinions (see, e.g., Dolbeare and Hammond 1971; Rosenberg 1991; Spriggs 1996; Black et al. 2016).

We therefore argue that the majority will feel more pressured to respond to a clear, readable opinion than one that is dense and complex. Clearly written opinions are more likely to be understood by multiple audiences, from lower court judges to members of Congress to the media to the lay public. And, as the majority is also concerned with whether the dissent will receive external attention when calculating whether to respond, Justice Scalia's writing advice offers a cautionary reminder: "When you write well, you capture the attention of your audience much better than when you write poorly" (Garner 2010, 53).

To account for *Readability,* we use the Flesh-Kincaid grade-level readability measure. The Flesch-Kincaid grade-level measure is one of the most straightforward but also most reliable and widely used measures to assess how easily a text is understood by an average reader. It is based on the wordiness of the document as well as the complexity of the words used; a document that uses more words per sentence, and more words with a greater number of syllables, translates to a document that is more difficult to comprehend. The score itself is calculated to reflect the average number of years of formal education needed to read and understand the text.[1] We expect that dissents receiving a higher grade-level score will be less likely to be cited by the majority.

It is important to note that the words-per-sentence category is based on the number of times that end-of-sentence markers are detected, which includes all periods. One potential issue concerns the fact that judicial opinions contain common legal abbreviations and legal citations with multiple periods; text analysis software counts each period as the end of a sentence, even if that sentence only has a single letter. We thus removed the periods from common abbreviations and legal citations using a script created by a computer software developer. This script used pattern matching and regular expressions to identify and remove the embedded periods from the opinions. In our dataset, the minimum grade level for dissents was 5, and the maximum grade level was 29, with a mean of 13.

Second, we argue that good legal writing reflects analytical thinking. For legal professionals, words are the tools of the trade and in order to produce effective legal writing, communication skills are inseparable from analytic skills (Parker 1997). In fact, an important trait of a legal writer is that the writer possesses strong analytical skills: "[S]trong legal analysis permeates persuasive documents" (M. R, Smith 2008, 163).

To measure analytical thinking, we use the computer content program Linguistic Inquiry and Word Count (LIWC).[2] LIWC is a software program developed by psychologists to measure a variety of linguistic features, such as the expression of emotions, cognitive thought processes, and the use of pronouns (Tausczik and Pennebaker 2010). LIWC is a dictionary-based program, meaning that it contains lists of words that correspond to separate dictionaries that represent larger concepts. Dozens of studies have used indicators from LIWC to explain various phenomena, with these results demonstrating predictive validity. Moreover, the validity and reliability of LIWC's categories have been extensively tested by previous scholars (see, e.g., Pennebaker and King 1999; Tausczik and Pennebaker 2010).[3]

Our measure of *Analytic Writing* reflects a summary variable measured via LIWC that has been rescaled to reflect a 100-point scale ranging from 0 to 100 (Pennebaker et al. 2015). Numbers above 50 generally reflect formal, logical, and hierarchical thinking, while scores below 50 tend to reflect more informal, personal, and narrative styles. Analytic thinking has been linked to intelligence, better performance in college classes, and better education in high school (Jordan and Pennebaker 2016). Whereas analytic thinkers like to break down and analyze a problem, narrative thinkers generally prefer to relay their own experiences and tell stories to understand a problem (Jordan and Pennebaker 2016). Analytical thinking is indicated by the greater use of nouns, articles, and prepositions, while an informal manner of writing is reflected by using more pronouns, auxiliary verbs (e.g., is, have, was), and common adverbs (e.g., really, so, very) (Jordan and Pennebaker 2016). For example, LIWC was used to analyze the debates during the 2016 primaries, finding that "Clinton spoke in a formal, analytic style. She focused on her policy proposals and issues and laid them out in a logical fashion. Trump had a shoot-from-the-hip, informal way of speaking using stories and anecdotes to explain his thinking" (Jordan and Pennebaker 2016). Not surprisingly, dissents are generally written to reflect analytic thinking, with a mean value of 94, a minimum value of 58, and a maximum value of 99.

Third, we argue that strong legal writing depends on the persuasive citation of past precedents. The more a dissent is grounded in Supreme Court precedent, the more it signals the strength of the legal argument proposed by the dissent. Judges across the judicial hierarchy use precedent to explain and justify their decisions. They also use precedent strategically to signal to other judges and outside actors that the decision reached is correct and legitimate; this use of precedent is particularly important for a dissent seeking to urge fellow justices and external audiences that the majority's decision is incorrect. Conversely, an opinion referencing little precedent may suggest a weaker foundation for the opinion itself (see, e.g., Walsh 1997; Hume 2009).

To measure the extent to which the dissenting opinion is *Well Grounded in Precedent,* we count the number of Supreme Court cases cited by each dissent.[4] We performed a logarithmic transformation of the raw number to consider the possibility of diminishing returns for additional Supreme Court citations when there are already a substantial number of cases cited. The actual value was the natural log of 1+ the number of Supreme Court cases cited, since there were dissents that did not cite any Supreme Court precedent, and the natural log is undefined for zero. Before transforming the number of Supreme Court cases cited by the dissent, the values ranged from 0 to 128, with a mean of 10.5. After transforming the variables, the minimum value was 0, the maximum value was 4.9, with a mean of 2.03.

ATTENTION-GRABBING DISSENTS

The second component of our theory argues that the majority must consider the likelihood that outside actors will pay attention to the arguments offered in the dissent. The majority wishes to guard against backlash for its decision, and the existence of a dissent may increase the likelihood of such a negative response. But, as we argue throughout this book, not all dissents are created equal. Some will draw notice, and thus pose a potential threat to the strength and power of the majority opinion, while other dissents will simply fade away into obscurity. Dissents that draw notice, whether from external actors, the public or the media, may threaten the majority's position. Increased media attention can work to mobilize potential litigants to further pursue cases in certain areas (see, e.g., Baird 2004), draw attention to calls for Congress to statutorily override Supreme Court decisions (see, e.g., Hausegger and Baum 1999), or complicate lower court implementation (see, e.g., Peterson 1981). Much as with well-written dissents, attention-grabbing dissents can also push majority opinion writers to craft stronger, more persuasive majority opinions. Justice Ginsburg credited Justice Scalia's dissenting opinion in the *Virginia Military Institute* case for helping her improve the quality of her majority opinion in that case: "The final draft, released to the public, was ever so much better than my first, second, and at least a dozen more drafts, thanks to Justice Scalia's attention-grabbing dissent" (Ginsburg 2008, 6). We argue that certain factors may increase the probability of a dissent attracting external attention, thereby increasing the majority's need to publicly and forcefully address the dissent's claims.

Some of these factors relate to the writing of the opinion itself. Above we discussed how certain features of opinion writing might particularly appeal to fellow justices; here we focus on opinion-writing tools that might be more likely to attract attention from outside political actors, the media, or the public. Certain linguistic features may not fall into the "ideal" legal writing parameters, but they may be quite effective in terms of drawing public and media attention. As Justice Scalia aptly summarized, dissenting "makes the practice of one's profession as a judge more satisfying. To be able to write an opinion . . . to express precisely the degree of quibble, or foreboding, or disbelief, or indignation that one believes the majority's disposition should engender—that is indeed an unparalleled pleasure" (Scalia 1998, 22–23).

We draw from Justice Scalia's admission as to the freedom from constraints and even niceties that justices may revel in while writing a dissent to explore the linguistic features that justices may use to intentionally make their dissents more memorable and attention-worthy. First, while legal writing guides caution against the overuse of adjectives, adverbs, and intensifiers (see, e.g., Zinsser 1980; Strunk and White 1999), it is these components of writing that allow a justice to highlight the degree of concern she holds. Specifically, using adjectives and adverbs aids in providing details to describe a scene or a feeling, and using adjectives and adverbs (and even overusing them) is more likely to grab someone's attention.

Regarding the use of intensifiers, Lance N. Long and William H. Christensen (2013) present a theory of argumentative threat, or the notion that the use of intensifiers increases as the size of the perceived threat the author is addressing grows. Specifically, "[t]he idea is that those who agree with us are generally good, and therefore we use general terms indicating that their good acts pervade the entire group and are the norm. Conversely, a bad act is described with specificity so as to limit its application to the specific situation" (Long and Christensen 2013, 947). The authors examine United States Supreme Court dissenting opinions, finding that dissenting opinions contain more intensifiers than majority opinions. They conclude that "this increased use of intensifiers could be a form of linguistic intergroup bias in the sense that a dissenting judge, alienated from the majority, seeks to show that the dissenting argument is 'obviously,' 'clearly,' and 'wholly' superior to the opinion of what is now the dissenter's out-group. The increased use of intensifiers . . . could be a subconscious attempt at showing the 'strength' of the dissenter's argument" (948). Building on this reasoning, we argue that the majority will be cognizant of the likely external response to such argumentative threats, given their deviation from the norm of traditionally staid legal writing. We therefore expect that the majority coalition will thus be more likely to feel they must respond to dissents using a high degree of adjectives, adverbs, and intensifiers.

We again apply LIWC to capture the use of these linguistic features. We first created a custom dictionary in LIWC to measure the percentage of intensifier words in each dissenting opinion, and we added the most common intensifiers: very, obviously, clearly, patently, absolutely, really, plainly, undoubtedly, certainly, totally, simply, wholly, extremely, quite, blatantly, completely, and highly (see Long and Christensen 2008; Edwards 2010; Schiess 2017).[5] Additionally, we modified the adverbs category in LIWC, removing any previously listed intensifier; thus, this category reflects the percentage of adverbs in the dissenting opinion, excluding common intensifiers. We then used the category "adjectives" in LIWC, which provides the percentage of adjectives in the dissenting opinion. We added these three categories together to calculate the percentage of each dissent that contains adverbs, adjectives, and intensifiers. We then determined the mean score—what we call *Writing Style*—for all dissents. Our argument, however, is not that some dissents will simply use many intensifiers, but will rather use them to such a degree that their overuse attracts notice. We therefore transformed this measure of Writing Style to reflect whether the dissent used an average, above-average, or below-average number of intensifiers. The final step was thus to code each dissent as a 1 if its Writing Style score was more than one standard deviation above the mean (representing that the dissent used more than the average percentage of adverbs, adjectives, and intensifiers), -1 if the score was less than one standard deviation below the mean, and 0 if the score fell between one standard deviation of the mean in either direction (representing an average percentage of adverbs, adjectives, and intensifiers). The majority of dissents (73%) are written using an average percentage of adverbs, adjectives, and intensifiers, with 13 percent using less than average and 14 percent using more than the average percentage.

We also, returning to Justice Scalia's explanation, propose that dissents that utilize more negative emotional language than the average dissent will draw outside attention, and thus be more likely to provoke a response from the majority. On the one hand, good legal writing can include using emotive words that evoke a more sympathetic response to the writer's argument (Osbeck 2012, 452). On the other hand, Melvin I. Urofsky (2017, 13) maintains that many dissents are "matters of pique," and those dissents that use a "strident tone" will "cloud the intellectual argument" and thus have less of an impact in the constitutional dialogue. We contend, however, that while such language may be off-putting to one's colleagues (the focus of Urofsky's constitutional dialogue), it may instead have the propensity to draw increased external attention in the broader legal and policy dialogue we seek to understand. A recent study finds that negative, emotionally charged dissents attract more media coverage (Bryan and Ringsmuth 2016). Additionally, Rachael K. Hinkle and Michael J. Nelson (2018) find that dissents using more negative emotional language are cited more in future Supreme Court majority opinions.

We extend the arguments offered by both Amanda C. Bryan and Eve M. Ringsmuth (2016) and Hinkle and Nelson (2018) to the contemporaneous legal and policy debate. We argue that majority opinion writers will feel an increased threat from dissents that use a disproportionally high level of emotional language and specifically negative emotional language, and therefore be more likely to believe they must address these dissents to try to mitigate their broader effect on the legal and policy dialogue. We account for *Negative Emotional Language* following the measure developed by Bryan and Ringsmuth (2016), with a slight modification. Their measure uses LIWC's dictionary of negative words, with a few adjustments: it adds a few words used in the legal vernacular while also excluding those words that are legal "terms of art" (such as assault, exhaust, and victim) or profanities "that might make it into the facts of the case but are highly unlikely to have been used by the justices" (Bryan and Ringsmuch 2016, 168). We use their dictionary to calculate the percentage of negative words in each dissent. Our final measure, like that of Writing

Style, is calculated to reflect whether the percentage of negative words in each dissent was above the mean usage across all dissents; dissents with a negative language percentage more than one standard deviation above the mean are coded 1, more than one standard deviation below the mean are coded -1, and all others coded 0 to reflect an average percentage of negative words. This measure allows us to more accurately determine if a justice's negative emotional language usage was of a degree likely to attract outside attention. In our dataset, most dissents use the average percentage of negative emotional words (77%), with 9 percent using less than the average and 14 percent using more than the average.

Finally, in terms of opinion content, we account for the amount of *Distinctive Words* the dissent uses. Similar to the use of adjectives and adverbs as well as negative emotional language, we argue that dissents that use a disproportionate amount of distinct or memorable language will draw outside external attention. Here, we build on the arguments offered by Hinkle and Nelson (2018). Hinkle and Nelson examine the use of memorable language in dissents with respect to their effect on future Court majorities, but we argue that the same forces that may influence future justices likely influence the majority opinion writer in the same case. They used a rolling series of four-decade segments of dissents to build dynamic frequencies that were used to measure how distinctive words are over time. A distinctive word was any word in the bottom 10 percent of the relevant frequency distribution; the variable used by Hinkle and Nelson (2018) reflected the total number of occurrences of distinctive words in each dissent. We first modified that variable to be a percentage of the total words in the dissent, and then determined whether the percentage of distinctive words in each dissent was above the mean usage across all dissents. Dissents with distinctive percentage more than one standard deviation above the mean are coded 1, more than one standard deviation below the mean are coded -1, and all others coded 0 to reflect an average percentage of distinctive words. In our dataset, most dissents use the average percentage of distinctive words (77%), with 10 percent using less than the average and 13 percent using more than the average percentage.

CHARACTERISTICS OF DISSENT COALITION

We also, as explicated in more detail in the introduction, argue that certain characteristics of the dissent coalition might potentially draw sufficient outside attention to constitute a potential threat to the majority. We examine two facets of the dissent coalition. First, we examine the degree of ideological heterogeneity among the dissenting justices. Given that opinions provide ideological signals for liberal or conservative positions on issues, an opinion with a mixed ideological coalition suggests opposition to the majority position cannot be dismissed as simple ideological disagreement. Ideologically heterogeneous dissents should therefore hold greater weight, and draw more external attention, than one that is not. For example, a majority coalition of only conservatives might give more weight to a dissenting opinion that was supported by both liberals and conservatives as opposed to one simply supported by the ideological opposition. Consider the dissent issued by conservative Justice Scalia and liberal Justice Stevens in *Hamdi v. Rumsfeld* (2004). Justice Sandra Day O'Connor's plurality opinion not only cited their dissent but spent five paragraphs discussing it: "Scalia acknowledges. . . . Scalia relies. . . . Scalia cites. . . . Scalia accepts. . . . paradigm outlined by . . . Scalia. . . . Scalia envisions. . . . Scalia largely ignores. . . . Scalia refers to. . . . Scalia's treatment. . . . Scalia finds. . . . Scalia can point to. . . . Scalia presumably would. . . ." (542 U.S. 507). A heterogeneous dissenting coalition also arguably sends a more credible signal to outside observers, increasing the majority's motivation to explain why the majority is right and the dissent is wrong.

To measure the *Ideological Heterogeneity of the Dissenters,* we calculated the difference between the maximum and minimum Martin-Quinn (2002) score of the justices in the dissent and we expect that, as the ideological heterogeneity of the dissenting coalition increases, the majority opinion will be more likely to cite the dissent. The mean score for ideological heterogeneity is 1.9 with a low of 0 and a high of 10.5.

One potential concern, however, is that our measure of ideological heterogeneity may truly be capturing the effect of a related, but distinct variable: coalition size. Larger dissenting coalitions may also reflect increased ideological heterogeneity, but in certain periods, the dissenting coalition on the Court is both large and ideologically homogeneous. We therefore may inaccurately attribute the effect of coalition size to the ideological heterogeneity of the coalition. Furthermore, the larger the dissent coalition, the more likely it is to draw outside attention, as compared to an opinion issued by a single justice. Thus, we include a variable for the *Number of Dissenters* for each dissent, and we expect that as that number increases, the majority opinion will be more likely to cite the dissent. The number of dissenters ranges from 1 to 4, with a mean of 2.3. However, larger dissenting opinion coalitions are correlated with ideological heterogeneity at 0.64. We therefore estimate two separate models—Model 1 contains the variable for Ideological Heterogeneity while Model 2 includes the variable Number of Dissenters—in order to be able to discern the distinct effects each of these coalition characteristics may have on the majority's response to a dissent.

The second characteristic concerning the justices we include is the *Ideological Difference between the Majority and Dissent Coalition Medians,* using Martin-Quinn (2002) scores. When the majority and dissenting coalitions are ideologically disparate, it may be easier for the majority to simply dismiss the dissent's arguments as ideological or partisan pique. Alternatively, majority opinion writers may find more persuasive—or view as more threatening—a dissent written by those they view as ideologically compatible. External actors are similarly more likely to take notice when the majority and dissenting coalitions are ideologically similar. Thus, we expect that the closer the two coalitions are ideologically, the more likely the majority will cite the dissent. This variable ranges from 0 to 10.98, with a mean of 2.7.

ADDITIONAL CONTROL VARIABLES

Finally, we include a measure of how many days are left until the end of the Court's term. Studies of opinion writing find that as the end of term draw near, justices are less likely to write separate opinions given the lack of time (Maltzman, Spriggs, and Wahlbeck 2000; Collins 2011), and we argue similar end-of-term pressures may decrease how much attention majorities give to dissenting opinions. We use June 30 as the date for the end of the term and subtract the date of oral argument (or the date of reargument) for this variable—*Days Left until the End of Term.*[6] The minimum number of days is 22, the maximum number is 273, and the average number is 169. Table 2 provides the summary statistics of our independent variables.

Results

To examine the effects of a dissent on the majority opinion, we analyze the Supreme Court's dissenting opinions in all signed, orally argued decisions during the 1953–2004 terms.[7] The unit of analysis is the dissenting opinion, and the dependent variable is whether the majority or plurality opinion cited the dissent in the same case, reflecting 1 if the dissent was cited, and 0 otherwise.[8] We account for the possibility that variance in citing dissents might

TABLE 2. Summary statistics for independent variables

Variable	Mean	Median	SD	Min	25%	75%	90%	Max
Reading grade level	13.14	13.00	2.00	5.00	12.00	14.00	16.00	29.00
Analytic score	94.09	94.96	3.77	57.91	92.92	96.41	97.36	99.00
# of precedent (logged)	2.03	2.08	.97	0.00	1.39	2.77	3.22	4.86
Writing style	.010	0	.52	-1	0	0	1	1
Negative words	.042	0	.48	-1	0	0	1	1
Distinctive language	.020	0	.48	-1	0	0	1	1
Ideological heterogeneity	1.93	1.38	2.00	0	0	3.31	4.60	10.54
# of dissenters	2.33	2	1.07	1	1	3	4	4
Ideological difference	2.72	2.43	1.88	.001	1.27	3.83	5.32	8.40
Days until end of term	169.08	169	68.39	22	102	234	260	273

be due to shifts over time, and that certain majority opinion authors may be more likely to cite dissents than others, by estimating a multilevel model with random effects for term and for majority opinion author. Specifically, the majority opinion author is nested within the Court's annual terms. Since the dependent variable is dichotomous, we use a multilevel probit model.

Table 3 displays the parameter estimates for our model, indicating which factors increase or decrease the likelihood that the majority opinion will cite the dissent. Both Model 1 and Model 2 contain our fully specified model, with Model 1 including the ideological heterogeneity of the dissenters and Model 2 including the number of dissenters given their collinearity. The models are substantially similar, so we focus our discussion primarily on Model 1. The likelihood ratio test for both models shows that the random intercept model is statistically superior to the probit model, and that in order to correctly test our hypotheses of interest, we need to account for the variance that exists both over time and between different majority opinion authors.

TABLE 3. Multi-level probit model with random effects for majority opinion writer and term: Whether majority/plurality opinion cited dissent, 1953–2004

Variable	Model 1			Model 2		
	Coefficient	S.E.	p-value	Coefficient	S.E.	p-value
Well-Written Dissents						
Reading grade level of dissent	-0.019	0.015	0.192	-0.022	0.015	0.145
Analytically written dissent	0.018	0.008	0.027	0.017	0.008	0.047
Number of precedent (logged)	0.326	0.030	0.000	0.299	0.030	0.000
Attention-grabbing Dissents						
Writing style of dissent	0.121	0.055	0.027	0.119	0.055	0.031
Negative emotional words	0.077	0.057	0.176	0.076	0.057	0.187
Distinctive language	0.033	0.060	0.586	0.028	0.060	0.646

	Model 1			Model 2		
Dissent Coalition						
Ideological heterogeneity of Dissenters	0.084	0.014	0.000	--	--	--
Number of dissenters	--	--	--	0.204	0.026	0.000
Ideological difference between majority and dissent	-0.044	0.015	0.003	-0.038	0.015	0.012
Other						
Days until the end of term	0.001	0.000	0.003	0.001	0.000	0.002
Constant	-3.108	0.786	0.000	-3.206	0.788	0.000
Variance Components						
Term-level	0.787	0.185	--	0.744	0.188	--
Majority Opinion Writer-level	0.273	0.047	--	0.287	0.049	--

$N = 3684$; p-values based on two-tailed tests.

Model 1: LR test vs. probit model: chi2(2) = 594.78; Prob > chi2 = 0.000.

Model 2: LR test vs. probit model: chi2(2) = 586.05; Prob > chi2 = 0.000.

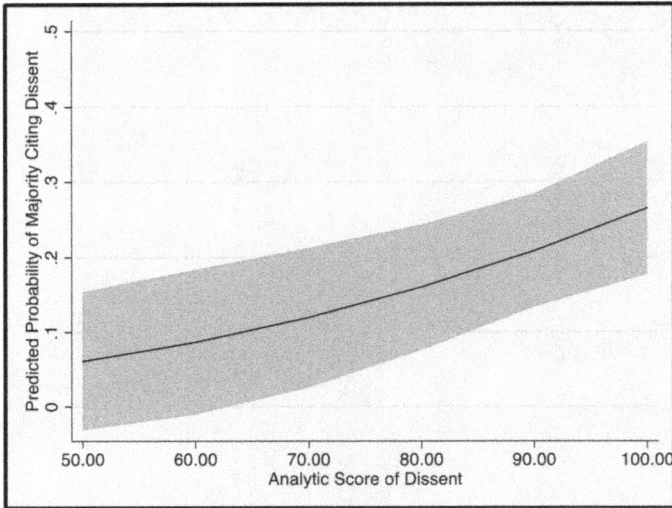

FIGURE 11. Probability of majority/plurality citing dissent in relation to analytic score of dissent

Overall, the results provide support for our theory that the majority is more likely to cite a dissent when it views the dissent as a potential threat. Is a well-crafted dissent more likely to be cited by the majority opinion in the same case than a less well-written dissent? Two of our strong writing variables are shown to be significant at $p<0.05$. First, the more analytically written the dissent, the more likely the majority opinion will cite the dissent. The predicted probability of a majority opinion citing a dissent, setting all continuous independent variables at their means and dichotomous variables to their modes, is 0.231. Figure 11 highlights the effect of an analytically written dissent on the probability of citation. The likelihood of citation by the majority increases by 9.09 percent (0.231 to 0.252) when the analytical score of the dissent increases from its mean to one standard deviation above the mean.

Second, dissents citing more precedent are more likely to be cited by the majority than those that are less grounded in precedent, with the likelihood of the majority citing the dissent increasing by 45.89 percent (0.231 to 0.337) when the number of precedents cited increases one standard deviation above the mean. Figure 12 graphically displays this relationship. Thus, it appears that the majority opinion writers respond to dissents that reflect formal, logical, and hierarchical thinking and those that cite more precedents.

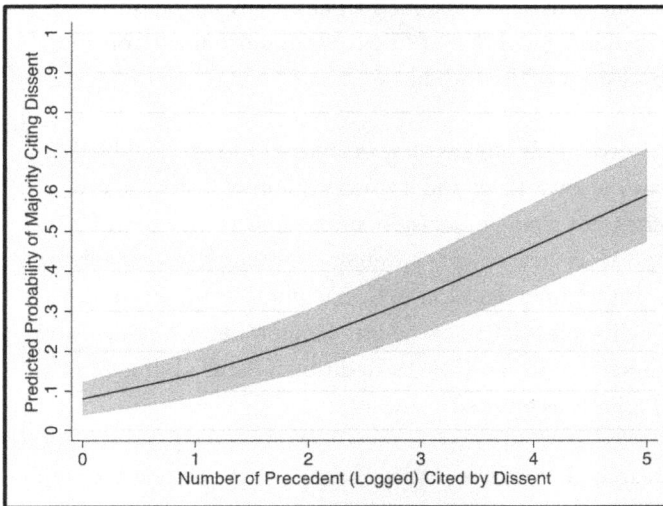

FIGURE 12. Probability of majority/plurality citing dissent in relation to number of precedent (logged) cited by dissent

For example, Justice Stevens's lengthy dissent in *Pennhurst v. Halderman* (1984) contained a whopping 116 Supreme Court precedents. Justice Lewis Powell's majority opinion spent ten pages—much of which are detailed discussions of precedents in footnotes—refuting Justice Stevens's opinion, taking note of both its size and its heavy reliance on prior decisions:

> The contrary view of Justice Stevens' dissent rests on fiction, is wrong on the law, and, most important, would emasculate the Eleventh Amendment.... We are prompted to respond at some length to Justice Stevens' 41-page dissent in part by his broad charge that 'the Court repudiates at least 28 cases.' The decisions the dissent relies upon simply do not support this sweeping characterization. . . . The dissent bases its view on numerous cases from the turn of the century and earlier. These cases do not provide the support the dissent claims to find. Many are simply miscited. (106–109) [citations omitted]

Similarly, in *Seminole Tribe v. Florida* (1996), Chief Justice William Rehnquist's majority opinion discussed Justice David Souter's dissent at length, both in multiple footnotes and over six pages in the main text of the opinion.

Because Justice Souter's dissent contained an unusually large number of Supreme Court precedents (101), Chief Justice Rehnquist spent considerable time attacking this aspect of the dissent:

> The dissent . . . disregards our case law in favor of a theory cobbled together from law review articles and its own version of historical events. The dissent cites not a single decision since *Hans* (other than *Union Gas*) that supports its view of state sovereign immunity, instead relying upon the now-discredited decision in *Chisholm v. Georgia*. Its undocumented and highly speculative extralegal explanation of the decision in *Hans* is a disservice to the Court's traditional method of adjudication. (68–69) [citations omitted]

Although research shows that justices write clearer majority opinions when they expect the least compliance and that circuit courts are more likely to comply with readable opinions (see, e.g., Black et al. 2016), it does not appear that the readability of a dissent influences whether the majority cites that dissent, although it is in the expected direction.

Are attention-grabbing dissents more likely to be cited by the majority opinion? As expected, the more adverbs, adjectives, and intensifiers the dissent contains, the more likely the majority will cite the dissent. When the percentage of this type of language is higher than average, the predicted probability of the majority citing the dissent is 0.269 whereas when the percentage is lower than average, the predicted probability drops to 0.196, a 27.14 percent decrease. Figure 13 graphically depicts this relationship between writing style of the dissent and citation by the majority. This result suggests that majorities may feel pressure to respond to dissents that vehemently disagree with the majority or strongly emphasize the potential consequences of the Court's decision.

For example, in *NLRB v. Allis-Chalmers Mfg. Co.* (1967), Justice Hugo Black, writing for his fellow dissenters William O. Douglas, John Marshall Harlan, and Potter Stewart, made clear through his word choices his grave misgivings with the Court's opinion. The case addressed whether a union was guilty of unfair labor practices under the National Labor Relations Act. Justice Black criticized the Court's interpretation of the act, noting the "emphatic guarantees of the Act" (199). He also ridiculed the Court's determination that certain words were ambiguous, arguing "any union official with sufficient intelligence and learning to be chosen as such could hardly fail to comprehend

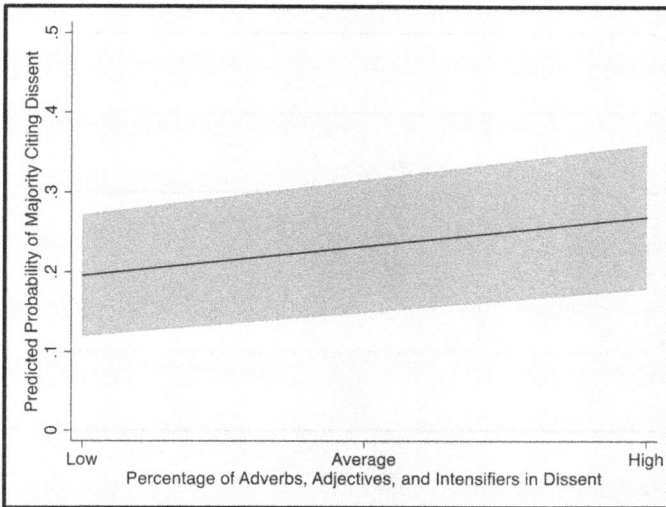

FIGURE 13. Probability of majority/plurality citing dissent in relation to writing style of dissent

the meaning of these plain, simple English words" (201). And he continued his assault on the Court's opinion by concluding that "the Court utilizes ambiguous, extemporaneous legislative comments to circumvent the unambiguous language of a carefully drafted statute" (212), using a number of adjectives to drive home his points. The majority found it necessary to respond to the dissent's arguments, including the dissent's charge that the Court relied on an "unarticulated premise that the Court has power to add a new weapon to the union's economic arsenal" (202; the majority responded to this charge in footnote 32).

We do not find, however, any effect for either negative emotional language or the use of distinctive language. The majority is no more or less likely to cite a dissent that utilizes these rhetorical flourishes. While prior research suggests that the media tend to be more likely to cover negative dissents, it does not appear that the majority opinion writer is likewise influenced. Similarly, though previous studies find that future majorities are more likely to cite dissents that use distinctive language (and we find the same in chapter 4), this is not true of one's contemporaneous colleagues.

Turning to the variables that reflect dissent coalition characteristics, we find that as the ideological heterogeneity of the dissenting coalition increases, the majority opinion is more likely to cite the dissent. Figure 14 shows the

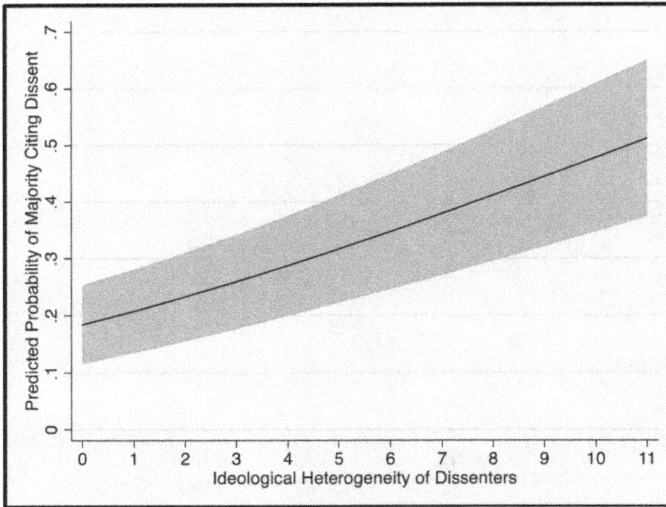

FIGURE 14. Probability of majority/plurality citing dissent in relation to ideological hetero-geneity of dissenters

predicted probability of citation over the values in the dataset. The predicted probability of citation increases by 23.38 percent (from 0.231 to 0.285) when ideological heterogeneity increases from its mean to one standard deviation above the mean. When the ideological heterogeneity variable is set at its minimum value, the predicted probability of citation is 0.184; when the variable is set at its maximum value, the predicted probability jumps to 0.496, an increase of 169.57 percent.

Consider *Metropolitan Life Insurance Co. v. Ward* (1985), where the Court's most ideologically liberal justices—Brennan and Marshall—joined conservative Justice Rehnquist in a dissent issued by Justice O'Connor. The majority cited their dissent twice, each time self-consciously defending its position: "As the dissent finds our failure to resolve whether Alabama may continue to collect its tax 'baffling,' we reemphasize the procedural posture of the case. . . . This case does not involve or question, as the dissent suggests, the broad authority of a State to promote and regulate its own economy" (479 U.S. 869, 875, 882) [citations omitted].

In Model 2, we include the number of dissenters joining each dissent. When there is one justice, the predicted probability of the majority citing the dissent is 0.154 whereas when there are four justices joining the dissent, the

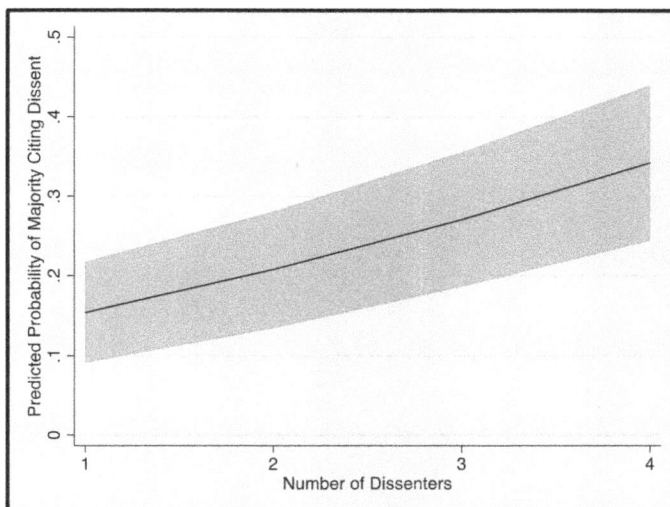

FIGURE 15. Probability of majority/plurality citing dissent in relation to number of dissenters joining each dissent

probability increases to 0.342, an increase of 122.08 percent. Figure 15 graphically displays this relationship. Both these measures capture a potential threat the majority may see as stemming from a dissent coalition that will likely draw external attention, whether due to its relative size or its coalition of legally strange bedfellows.

As expected, we also find that as the difference between the median of the majority coalition and the dissent coalition increases, indicating that the justices on either side are ideologically disparate, the majority opinion is less likely to cite the dissent. When the ideological difference between the majority and the dissent increases from its mean to one standard deviation above the mean, the predicted probability of the majority citing the dissent decreases from 0.231 to 0.206, a decrease of 10.82 percent. Figure 16 shows the predicted probability of citation over the values in the dataset.

Finally, time is a factor when revising the majority opinion to respond to the dissent. As the number of days until the end of term increases, the majority opinion is more likely to cite the dissent. Conversely, as the end of the term nears, the majority opinion is less likely to cite the dissent. Figure 17 illustrates this relationship. This result is not surprising given that chambers are under considerable pressure to complete opinions before the Court adjourns for the

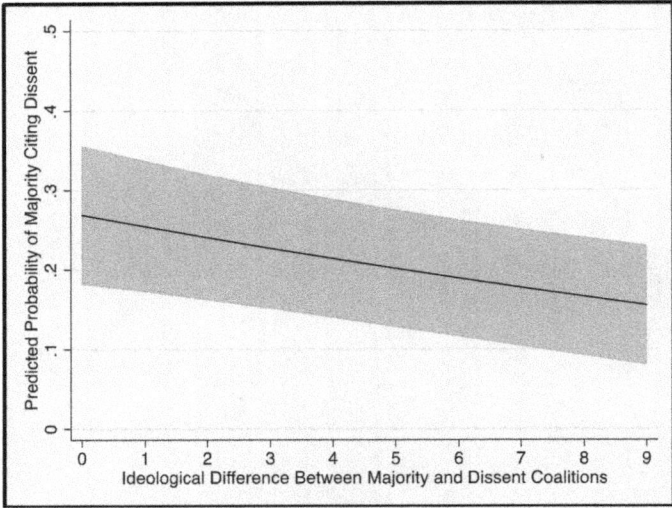

FIGURE 16. Probability of majority/plurality citing dissent in relation to ideological difference between majority and dissent coalitions

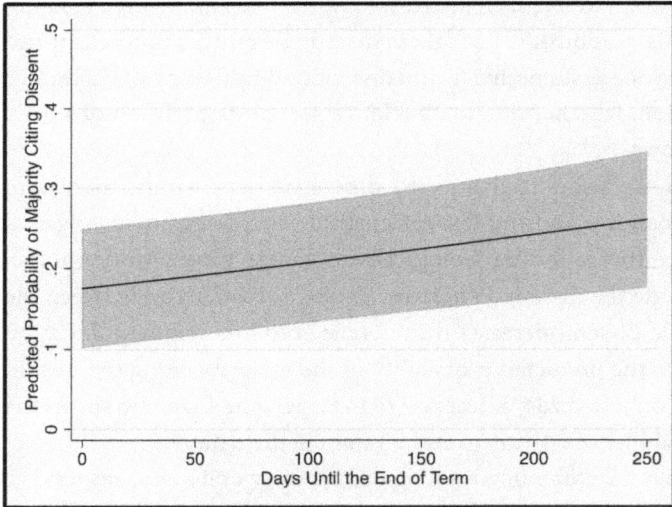

FIGURE 17. Probability of majority/plurality citing dissent in relation to number of days until the end of term

summer. Justice Powell wrote his law clerks on June 23, 1984: "We are witnessing the usual June-end 'rush to judgment' that often leads to poorly written opinions and even errors."[9]

Discussion and Conclusion

In this chapter we explore what differentiates dissents that attract attention from the majority from those that are likely to fade into obscurity. Why does the majority respond to certain dissents by citing them in the majority opinion while ignoring others? Overall, we find that majority opinion authors are more likely to cite dissents that appear to pose an increased threat to the majority's position. What types of dissents are more likely to pose a threat? Our results reveal that majorities respond to both well-crafted dissents as well as those that are more likely to draw external notice. Dissents that reflect analytical thinking and those that are well grounded in precedent are more likely to be cited by the majority as well as dissents that grab attention by their higher than average use of adverbs, adjectives, and intensifiers. These results suggest that the majority is both persuaded by thoughtful and careful arguments made by their dissenting colleagues, while also cognizant of the need to defend its stance against a minority opinion crafted with the goal of appealing to external actors, the media, and/or the public.

The majority also responds to the composition of the dissenting coalition, with the majority more likely to cite a dissent when the justices are ideologically heterogeneous. The majority is similarly more likely to cite dissents reflecting large, rather than small, coalitions. In both cases, the majority likely recognizes that the configuration of dissenters will potentially gain outside attention, attention that increases the pressure on the majority to address the dissent and its arguments head-on. However, when the majority and dissenting coalitions are ideologically divergent—that is, when the dissent is more likely based on typical ideological disagreements—the majority is less likely to cite the dissent.

Overall, our findings reveal that certain types of dissents are influential in an immediate sense as majority opinion writers regularly cite and engage with dissenting opinions crafted in a particular way and comprised of particular justices. The dissents that are cited, nay highlighted, by the majority become a more concrete and public part of the broader legal and policy dialogue. And these dissents are those that the majority believes are most likely to pose a threat to the strength and power of the Court's opinion. A well-written and precedent-grounded dissent may sway lower court judges, while one that uses intensifiers may capture the attention of members of Congress, potential future litigants, and the public. And the media is most likely to pay attention to cases where an interesting story about the Court can be written, whether due to unusual justice combinations or large dissenting coalitions.

These results enable us to take the first step in explaining the intra-Court impact of dissents. And they highlight how accounting for certain dissent characteristics is essential to understand how dissents that accompany the majority opinion can shape the content of that majority opinion. Furthermore, the majority opinion is the Court's official entry into the broader legal and policy conversation. While dissents are publicly released, their effect is potentially ephemeral. But when the majority decides to embed the dissent's arguments directly into the majority opinion, the dissent now plays a more forceful and long-lasting role in the legal and policy discussion. Understanding when and why that happens is thus essential to understanding the full scope of the role the Court plays in crafting national law and policy. We turn in the next chapter to the question of when future Court majorities rely on past dissents, further bringing dissents into the ongoing legal and policy dialogue.

4 | Judicial Conversations through Time

The Influence of Dissents on Future US Supreme Court Majority Opinions

PRIOR TO *LINKLETTER v. Walker* (1965), new constitutional rules were generally applied retroactively to criminal defendants. However, the *Linkletter* Court refused to give *Mapp v. Ohio* (1961) — a case where the Court held that all evidence obtained by searches and seizures in violation of the Federal Constitution is inadmissible in a state criminal trial — retroactive effect, applying a three-pronged analysis to the retroactivity issue: (1) the purpose to be served by the new rule; (2) the amount of law enforcement dependence on the old rule; and (3) how retroactive application of the new rule may affect the ability of the criminal justice system to operate.

In *Desist v. United States* (1969), the Supreme Court, applying the three-pronged approach from *Linkletter,* held that new rules governing the admissibility of evidence obtained through electronic surveillance would only apply prospectively. Justice John M. Harlan II dissented, declaring: "'Retroactivity' must be rethought" (258). He argued that "all 'new' rules of constitutional law must, at a minimum, be applied to all those cases which are still subject to direct review by this Court at the time the 'new' decision is handed down" (258). According to Justice Harlan, it is essential to the integrity of the judicial process that all cases be resolved in light of the Court's best understanding of the Constitution and thus deciding that a new constitutional rule does not apply to a case before the Court on direct review disregards the current law. Justice Harlan likened the Court selectively applying new constitutional rules to an assertion of legislative power. Additionally, Justice Harlan argued that granting retroactive application of new rules to some defendants but not others violates the principle of treating similarly situated defendants the same. Justice Harlan's dissent has been positively cited nine times by later Supreme Court majority opinions.

For example, in *United States v. Johnson* (1982), the majority opinion discussed Justice Harlan's "comprehensive analysis" of retroactivity (546) for three pages, agreed that "'[r]etroactivity' must be rethought" (548), and ultimately "embrac[ed] Justice Harlan's views in *Desist*" (562). Similarly, in *Shea v. Louisiana* (1985), the Court had to decide whether to apply a new constitutional rule to cases then pending on direct appeal. The Court applied the new rule retroactively, noting: "The Court in *Johnson* found persuasive Justice Harlan's earlier reasoning that application of a new rule of law to cases pending on direct review is necessary in order for the Court to avoid being in the position of a super-legislature, selecting one of several cases before it to use to announce the new rule and then letting all other similarly situated persons be passed by unaffected and unprotected by the new rule" (56). The majority opinion in *Griffith v. Kentucky* (1987) cited Justice Harlan's dissent from *Desist* as well: "In Justice Harlan's view, and now in ours, failure to apply a newly declared constitutional rule to criminal cases pending on direct review violates basic norms of constitutional adjudication" (322).

Justices are not legally required to cite the content of a dissent, especially when that dissent comes from a prior case. As illustrated in figure 10 (chapter 3), majorities many times do not discuss a dissent filed in the current case. From 1953 through 2004 terms, approximately a quarter of dissents were cited by contemporaneous majorities, though the practice has become more common in recent years. It is even more rare for a subsequent Court to cite a past dissent. Citing a past dissent thus takes on enormous weight. When a Court majority cites a past dissent, and particularly when it cites a past dissent positively, that dissent becomes enshrined in the current legal and policy debate. The citation of past dissents in future cases shows that some dissents are not merely expressions of personal pique (see, e.g., Urofsky 2017), but rather important contributions to the justices' internal discourse as well as the broader legal and policy dialogue. And, in some cases, such as with Justice Harlan's dissent in *Desist,* the dissenting justice's contribution may eventually be adopted as the opinion of the Court. Other dissents, however, are never cited by a future Court, nor even discussed by the majority in the controlling case. What explains why Justice Harlan's dissent become part of the later debate over retroactivity? This chapter investigates this important question.

Heeding Past Calls: When Do Justices Cite Prior Dissents?

In chapter 3, we investigated the influence of a number of factors on the likelihood of the majority opinion citing the dissent that accompanied the majority opinion. In this chapter, we assess the influence of dissents in future cases. As discussed in the introduction, many dissents are written with an eye toward external actors and future Courts, with the real influence of a dissent "com[ing] later, often in shaping . . . the course of the law" (Urofsky 2017, 17). Dissenters are engaging in a public conversation over the meaning of the law (Urofsky 2012, 926), but sometimes those responding may not do so until many years in the future. It took over a decade before Justice Harlan's pleas were answered by future members of the Court.

What causes a dissent to be read by future members of the Court? And, more important, what causes these future justices to positively cite this dissent while deciding a future case? "Unlike majority opinions, [dissents] need not be read after the date of their issuance. They will not be cited, and will not be remembered, unless some quality of thought or of expression commends them to later generations" (Scalia 1998, 23). Similar to Justice Antonin Scalia's postulation, we argue that well-crafted and attention-grabbing dissents are more likely to have long-lasting jurisprudential value.

As explicated in the introduction and tested in chapter 3, we argue that contemporaneous dissents are more likely to be cited by the majority when they pose more of a threat to the majority. We contend that well-crafted and attention-grabbing dissents pose the most threat to the majority, and thus are the more likely to compel a response from the majority. Future courts face a different calculation: they are deciding whether to positively cite a past dissent, and to potentially use or adopt the reasoning of that dissent. Future courts are therefore not assessing whether the prior dissent poses a potential threat to the Court, but rather whether the dissent can aid the current majority. As Justice Scalia noted, however, a future justice will not notice or remember a past dissent without "some quality of thought or of expression."

We therefore argue that future courts will be more likely to cite those prior dissents that reflect writing characteristics that make them more persuasive and memorable. Specifically, we propose that such dissents are well crafted, using readable, analytic language, and are well grounded in precedent. As Chief Justice John Roberts explained, "We pick up the books in our chambers, and you get a case from 1872 or whenever it is, and you want to read it and understand what their view of the law was and what the precedent means. And if it is poorly written, sometimes you just kind of throw your hands up and look for something else" (Garner 2010, 8). Justices therefore look for past opinions that not only buttress their potential arguments, but also provide a high-quality, well-crafted argument.

More memorable dissents are also those that draw attention through the heightened use of negative emotional language; adjectives, adverbs, and intensifiers; and distinctive vocabulary. Andrew J. W. Civettini and David P. Redlawsk (2009) propose that people are more likely to remember information from political campaigns that prompts an emotional response. Studies in a wide variety of disciplines further find that people remember more easily information that stimulates negative, rather than positive, emotions (see e.g., D'Argembeau and Van der Linden 2005). Both emotional language and the use of intensifiers, which are many times designed to provoke an emotional reaction, may similarly aid recall. Studies in multiple areas find that the use of less common words aid memory as well (see e.g., Danescu-Niculescu-Mizil et al. 2012). We propose that each of these characteristics increases the likelihood of a dissent being potentially recalled, read, and ultimately included in the future legal and policy dialogue.

Data and Methods

To examine the effects of a dissent on future Supreme Court majority opinions, we again analyze the Supreme Court's dissenting opinions in all signed, orally argued decisions during the 1953–2004 terms. We then merge these opinions with a dataset that includes whether the dissent is ever cited in each subsequent term by a majority opinion.[1] Thus, our unit of analysis is the dissent-term, covering 1953 to 2014, and the dependent variable is whether the dissent received a non-negative citation by a majority opinion in that term. By using the dissent-term as the unit of analysis, we control for both the age of a dissent and the relevant political and institutional context. We use a multi-level probit model with random effects for dissenter, which further allows us to take into account the possibility that dissents written by specific justices are more or less likely to be cited in the future (see Hinkle and Nelson 2018). The likelihood ratio test shows that, mirroring chapter 3, the random intercept model is statistically superior to the probit model. Not surprisingly, dissents are rarely cited in a non-negative way by future majority opinions. Out of 131,182 dissent-term observations, only 1,032 observations (0.8%) are coded 1, meaning that the dissent received a non-negative citation during that term. The number of times a dissent is cited by a majority opinion during a term over the time period ranges from 0 to 9.

We employ the same independent variables used in chapter 3: *Grade Readability Level of Dissent, Analytic Writing, Number of Precedents Cited by the Dissent* (logged), *Writing Style* (adverbs, adjectives, and intensifiers), *Negative Emotional Language, Distinctive Words, Ideological Heterogeneity of Dissenters,* and the *Number of Dissenters*. Larger dissenting opinion coalitions tend to have more ideological heterogeneity and the variables are correlated at 0.63; thus, we again estimate two separate models, with Ideological Heterogeneity contained in Model 1, and Number of Dissenters contained in Model 2. We also include additional variables to account for the somewhat altered context of considering future citation practices.

To our knowledge, there is only one study that examines whether future majority opinions cite past dissents. Rachael K. Hinkle and Michael J. Nelson (2018) argue that dissenting justices who use more memorable language are more likely to achieve a long-lasting impact. They use "distinctive language" and "negative emotional language" to tap into the idea of memorable language. However, they do not take into account other characteristics of dissenting opinions, such as those we include to capture both well-crafted and attention-grabbing dissents. Additionally, that study does not include the previous treatment of the dissent, as we describe below. We therefore expand on their initial study to more comprehensively assess both what influences these majority-citing processes as well as the role of dissents in influencing the broader legal and policy debate. Our research design provides an opportunity to further our understanding of how dissents contribute to the conversation among the justices over time.

PREVIOUS TREATMENT OF DISSENT

In the previous chapter, our dependent variable was whether the majority cited the accompanying dissent. Here, we include that variable as an independent variable, and we expect dissents that already became part of the dialogue by being cited in the original majority opinion are more likely to be cited by future majority opinions. We code this variable (*Majority Cited the Dissent*) 1 if the original majority cited the dissent, and 0 otherwise.

We also include the number of times the Court's majority opinions cited the dissent in a non-negative manner through the years prior to the one under consideration. As the dissent becomes more enmeshed in the Court's discourse over the years, especially by members of the majority coalition, the more likely the dissent in question will continue to be a part of that conversation. We therefore expect that as the number of prior non-negative citations increases, so too will the likelihood of the Court's citing that dissent in subsequent years. The mean number of *Cumulative Prior Positive Citations of Dissent* is 0.201, with a minimum value of 0 and a maximum value of 9.

ADDITIONAL CONTROL VARIABLES

An important predictor of whether a past dissent is cited is the ideological position of the current Court. Many times, dissenters reflect ideological outliers—as discussed in chapter 1, the dissenting coalition of Justices Oliver Wendell Holmes and Louis Brandeis routinely stood apart from their colleagues throughout the 1920s. Over time, however, the ideological position of the Court shifts, perhaps becoming closer to that of the original dissenting justice. We thus expect that a future Court is more likely to favorably cite a particular dissent if the dissent author is ideologically similar to the current Court majority, and is less likely to do so when the dissent author is ideologically distant. We control for the ideological distance between the median of the Court in a given term and the author of the dissenting opinion, expecting that as the distance increases, the probability of a majority opinion citing the dissent will decrease. The mean *Ideological Distance between the Dissenting Author and Current Court Majority* is 2.1999, with a minimum value of 4.77e-10 and a maximum value of 8.669.

Whether a particular dissent is cited in the future is also dependent upon the issues the Court decides to hear each term. If the Court declines to accept any cases that address the same legal issues as the prior case, then it is basically impossible for that dissent to be cited that term. Alternatively, if the Court accepts a large number of cases in a particular issue area, then the number of opportunities for a prior dissent in that area to be cited necessarily increases (see Hinkle and Nelson 2018). We control for the proportion of the Court's docket in each term that addresses the same issue area (*Proportion of Same Issue Area on Docket*) as the dissent in question. The mean is 0.154, with a minimum value of 0 and a maximum value of 0.367.

Additionally, we control for the *Age of a Dissent* and its *Age Squared* and *Age-Cubed* (see Carter and Signorino 2010). It is well known that precedents depreciate over time, and so older precedents are less likely to be cited in the future than more recent precedents (Spriggs and Hansford 2001; 2002; Hansford and Spriggs 2006; Black and Spriggs 2013). We apply the same logic to dissents, and expect that older dissents are less likely to be cited in the future than more recent dissents. The mean age is 20.912, with a minimum age of 1 and a maximum of 61.

Finally, we control for whether the majority opinion that accompanied the dissent was overruled (coded 1 if *Overruled*, 0 otherwise). As we explained in the introduction, if the majority opinion was overruled in a previous case, there is less of a need for a future majority opinion to cite the prior dissent in that case. Instead, the majority opinion will simply cite the new, overruling majority opinion. For example, after *Bowers v. Hardwick* (1986) was overruled by *Lawrence v. Texas* (2003), there was no need to cite Justice Stevens's dissent in *Bowers* in future cases; instead, majority opinions could now cite the controlling precedent *Lawrence.*

Results

The empirical results displayed in table 4 show support for a number of our hypotheses. Both Model 1 and Model 2 contain our fully specified model, with Model 1 including ideological heterogeneity of the dissenting coalition members and Model 2 including number of dissenters given their collinearity. The model results are substantially similar, so we focus our discussion on Model 1.

Overall, the results provide support for our theory that well-crafted and attention-grabbing dissents are more likely to be cited in the future than dissents that are not. Intriguingly, however, we also find that what matters in terms of being well written and attention grabbing differs in some important ways between contemporaneous Courts and future Courts.

First, similar to our findings in chapter 3, we find that dissents that are well grounded in precedent are more likely to be cited by a future majority opinion. The baseline probability of the dissent being cited is 0.003 (with all independent variables set to their means if continuous, or to their modes if dichotomous). When the number of precedents cited by the dissent is set to one standard deviation above the mean, the predicted probability of citation by a future Court in a particular term doubles to 0.006. "To understand these numbers, it is important to appreciate that what may seem like small values of the probabilities can have overwhelming importance in substantive analyses of genuine rare-events data" (King and Zeng 2001, 711). For example, given our overall dataset of 131,193 dissent-term observations, the effect of this variable across the entire population of cases reflects an additional 393 times when a past dissent would be cited by a future majority, almost a third of our total number of observed future citation instances. Figure 18 illustrates this relationship. Given that *stare decisis* is regularly invoked by the justices to justify their decisions, it is not surprising that majority opinion writers would be more influenced by past dissents that are rife with citations to precedent.

TABLE 4. Multi-level probit model with random effects for dissenter: Whether a majority opinion cited the dissent in each subsequent term through 2014

Variable	Model 1			Model 2		
	Coefficient	S.E.	p-value	Coefficient	S.E.	p-value
Well-Crafted Dissents						
Reading grade level of dissent	0.022	0.007	0.002	0.022	0.007	0.002
Analytically written dissent	-0.008	0.004	0.035	-0.008	0.004	0.035
Number of precedent cited by dissent (logged)	0.259	0.015	0.000	0.259	0.015	0.000
Attention-grabbing Dissents						
Writing style of dissent	0.081	0.027	0.002	0.082	0.027	0.002
Negative emotional words	0.032	0.029	0.275	0.032	0.029	0.275
Distinctive language	0.068	0.029	0.022	0.068	0.029	0.022
Dissent Coalition						
Ideological Heterogeneity of Dissent	0.001	0.007	0.901	--	--	--
Number of Dissenters	--	--	--	0.002	0.012	0.861

Previous treatment of dissent

Previous treatment of dissent						
Whether contemporary majority cited dissent	0.025	0.028	0.372	0.024	0.028	0.380
Cumulative prior positive citations of dissent	0.192	0.015	0.000	0.192	0.015	0.000
Other						
Ideological distance between Court median and dissent	-0.051	0.010	0.000	-0.051	0.010	0.000
Prop. Of Same Issue Area on Docket	0.249	0.144	0.084	0.247	0.144	0.086
Age of Dissent	-0.041	0.007	0.000	-0.041	0.007	0.000
Age-Squared	0.000	0.000	0.541	0.000	0.000	0.539
Age-Cubed	2.16e-06	5.34e-06	0.686	2.14e-06	5.34e-6	0.689
Contemporary Majority Opinion Overruled	-0.185	0.116	0.111	-.184	0.116	0.111
Constant	-2.058	0.905	0.000	-2.059	0.345	0.000
Variance Component						
Dissenter-level	0.007	0.004	--	0.007	x	0.004

N = 131,182; p-value based on two-tailed test.

Model 1: LR test vs. probit model: chi2(2) = 14.69; Prob > chi2 = 0.0001.

Model 2: LR test vs. probit model: chi2(2) = 14.69; Prob > chi2 = 0.0001.

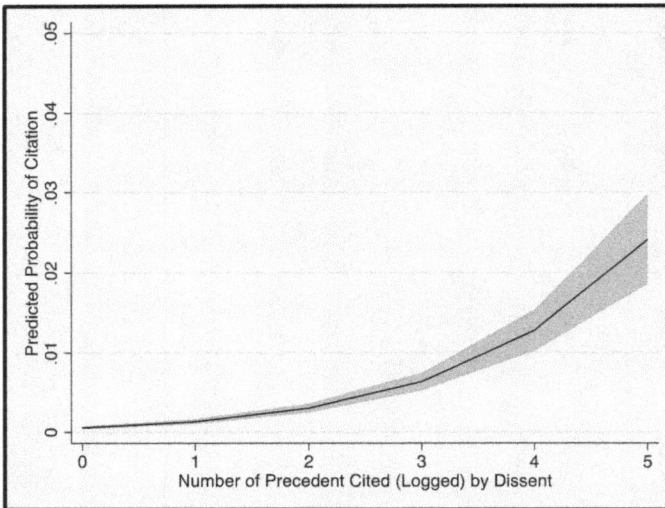

FIGURE 18. Probability of citation in the future in relation to number of precedent cited (logged) by dissent

Interestingly, the coefficients for both analytic language and the grade level of the dissent are in the opposite direction than expected, suggesting that dissents that are more analytical are less likely to be cited in the future and dissents that are more difficult to read are more likely to be cited in the future.

Why might future majority opinions prefer to cite dissents written at a higher grade level? Although there are studies that show readability increases lower court compliance (see, e.g., Black et al. 2016), the audience that is deciding whether (and how) to use a dissent in a majority opinion are Supreme Court justices. One potential explanation is that an opinion that is written at a higher grade level is arguably more sophisticated, and thus more likely to show off the "quality of thought" Justice Scalia suggested dissents need to grab the attention of future justices. Justices writing for other justices appears to be effective, particularly if justices are writing to persuade future colleagues on the errors of past Courts.

Alternatively, we find that the more analytically written the dissent, the less likely that dissent will be cited in the future. A low analytical score means not that the opinion is devoid of analysis, but rather that the opinion is written in a more narrative style. Narrative writing focuses on storytelling, and the writing is both less formal and more personal. While in chapter 3 we find logical persuasion may influence one's contemporaneous colleagues, a narrative style may increase the likelihood of future recall, and thus heighten the possibility of a future colleague remembering and using the dissent in a future case. For example, a study of physician recall of new opioid guidelines finds much higher recall when the information is presented in a narrative style rather than simply summarized in a more traditional, formal (e.g., analytical) style (Kilaru et al. 2014). Similarly, analyses of television and newspaper news stories find recall and comprehension is heightened when stories are presented in a narrative structure (see, e.g., Thorndyke 1979; Van Dijk 1983). And a very recent meta-analysis of comprehension and recall studies finds both comprehension and recall increase when individuals read a narrative, as opposed to expository, text (Mar et al. 2021). Our results, similar to these other studies of recall and writing style, thus suggest that how a justice frames her dissent may have important implications for whether that dissent becomes embedded in the Court's internal, and public-facing, dialogue. While one's contemporaneous peers are more persuaded by logical, expository writing, justices who endeavor to persuade future colleagues to adopt their arguments—and, by definition, need these colleagues to both recall and comprehend these past writings—may benefit from a deliberate use of a more narrative style.

We also find support for the proposition that more attention-grabbing dissents are more likely to be cited by future Court majorities. First, mirroring our results in chapter 3 for contemporaneous Courts, when the dissent uses a higher-than-average percentage of adverbs, adjectives, and intensifiers, the predicted probability of the dissent being cited by a majority opinion in the future increases from 0.003 to 0.004, an increase of 33.33 percent, or approximately 131 additional future citations across the entire sample (i.e., about 10% of all observed future citations). Figure 19 illustrates this relationship. This result again suggests that justices recall and respond when their past colleagues emphasize and embellish their concerns with the Court's majority opinion.

We additionally find that memorable language matters when assessing the effect of dissents on future Courts. The results reveal that the greater use of distinctive words in a dissent increases the probability of future citation. When the distinctive language used increases to one standard deviation above the mean, the predicted probability of future citation increases 33.33 percent (from 0.003 to 0.004); this result again suggests an increase of approximately 131 future citations across the entire sample. Figure 20 displays this relationship. This finding, coupled with the nonfinding in chapter 3 for this same variable, suggests that the function of memorable and distinctive language is primarily forward-looking. Memorable language taps into that

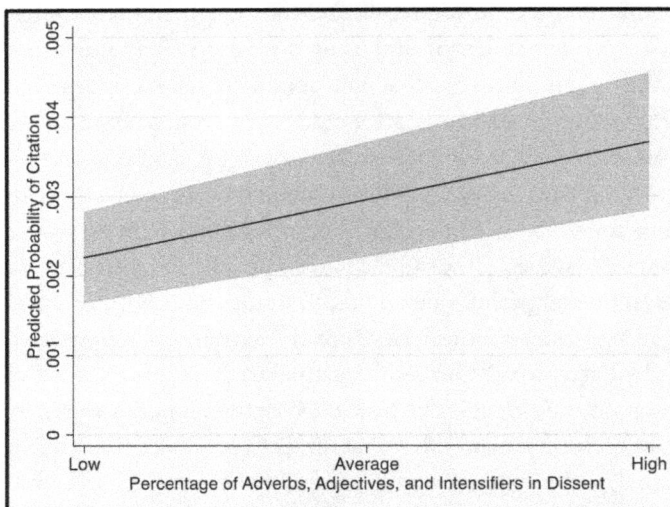

FIGURE 19. Probability of citation in the future in relation to writing style of dissent

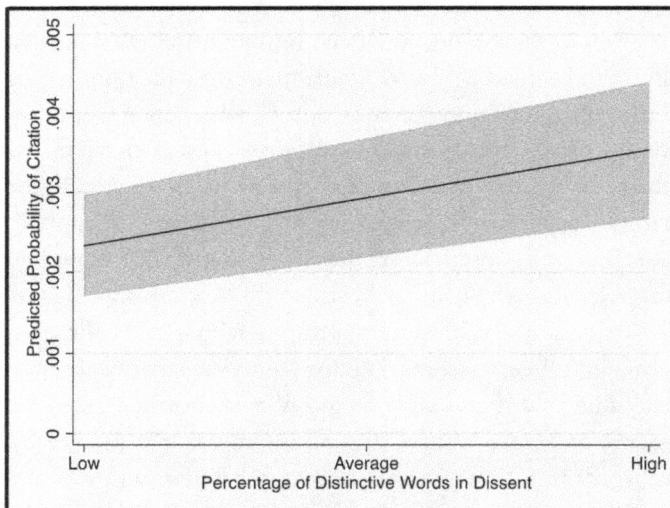

FIGURE 20. Probability of citation in the future in relation to distinctive words in dissent

unique "expression of thought" Justice Scalia noted is necessary for a dissent to be recalled and added into the justices' continuing dialogue. The dissenters know they have lost the current battle, and our findings reveal that writing for future battles is a successful strategy.

Although we found in the previous chapter that when the dissenting coalition is more ideologically heterogeneous (or when the number of justices increases) the majority opinion in that case is more likely to cite the dissent, the same does not appear to be true for future majority opinions. This finding may reflect the reality that while contemporaneous majority coalition justices must be concerned with the attention ideological heterogeneity or a large dissenting bloc may draw, few are likely to remember (or even care) about such justice pairings in the future. Rather, the attention is given to the content and style of the dissent itself.

However, as shown in figure 21, as the ideological distance between the median of the Court in a given term and the author of a past dissenting opinion increases, the probability of citation decreases, moving from 0.004 to 0.002 (or a decrease of approximately 262 total future citations across the sample) as the distance grows from one standard deviation below the mean to one standard deviation above the mean. Past dissent authors are therefore much more likely to have their entreaties heeded when the current Court majority

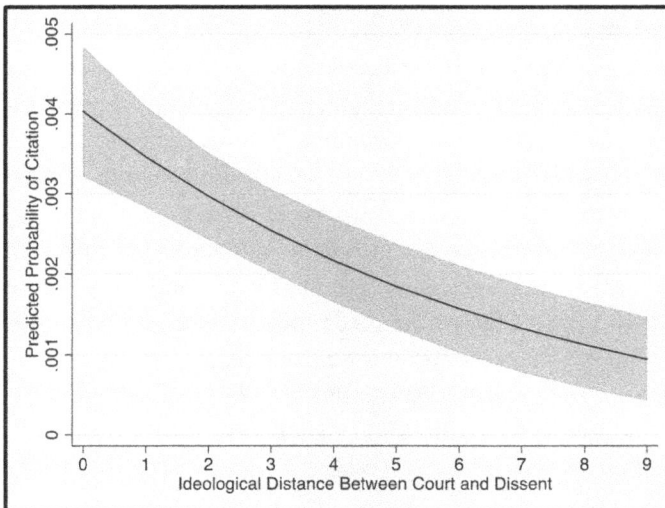

FIGURE 21. Probability of citation in the future in relation to ideological distance between the Supreme Court and dissent author

is ideologically aligned with their views. And the potential long-term jurisprudential impact of a dissent is greatly affected by changes over time in the
Court's ideological majority. While a justice at one time may be an ideological
outlier—such as Justice John Marshall Harlan, who famously dissented in
Plessy v. Ferguson (1896) and the *Civil Rights Cases* (1883)—in future years
and even decades past their demise, the views of that justice may reflect those
of the current Court. Justices thus write to try to persuade their contemporaneous colleagues to change their minds, and to state publicly their concerns
with the Court's decision, but they also write with the hope of future justices
heeding their calls.

Turning to the previous treatment of the dissent, we find mixed results.
Whether the original majority cited the dissent does not correlate with
whether the dissent is cited in the future. On the other hand, prior positive
citations of the dissent—the vitality of the dissent—significantly increases
the probability of being cited in subsequent majority opinions. If, in previous
years, the dissent has not been cited, the probability of a majority opinion
citing the dissent in the next year is 0.003. If the dissent has been cited once
in any previous year, the probability increases to 0.005, and if the dissent has
been cited two times in the previous years, the probability increases to 0.008.
In terms of future citation counts across the sample, a single prior citation increases the number of future citations by 262; two prior citations increase the
number of future citations by an additional 655 from the baseline. Figure 22
graphically depicts this relationship.

Finally, figure 23 graphically depicts the relationship between the age of a
dissent and whether a future majority opinion cites it. As expected, while exceptions such as Justice Harlan's famous dissent in *Plessy* exist, newer dissents
are much more likely to be recalled and cited by a future Court than older
dissents. The predicted probability of a more recent dissent (approximately
seven years old, which is one standard deviation below the mean) being cited
is nine times higher than an older dissent (set at 35, one standard deviation
above the mean). Thus, while future Courts do look to their past colleagues
for guidance, the impact of a dissent on the future dialogue is more likely
when the dissent was written relatively recently.

Discussion and Conclusion

In this chapter, we explore what factors influence whether future majority
opinions cite dissents from past cases. Our results show once again that not

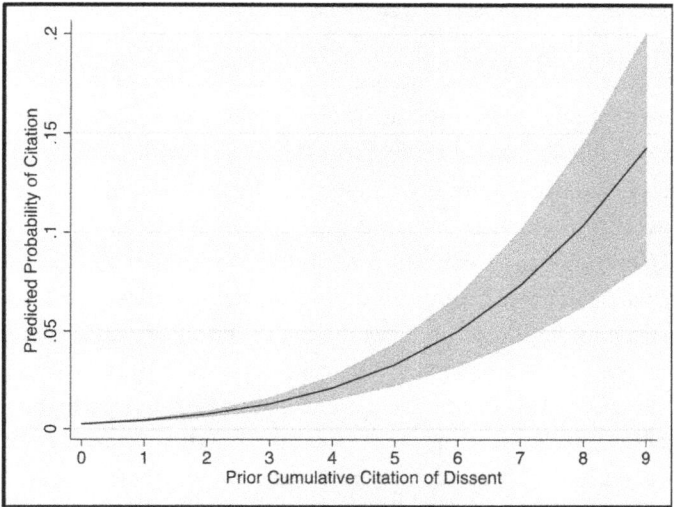

FIGURE 22. Probability of citation in the future in relation to cumulative prior citations of dissent

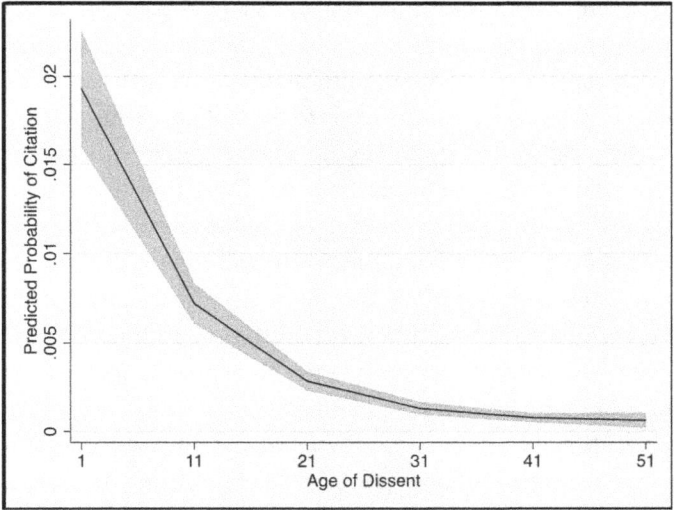

FIGURE 23. Probability of citation in the future in relation to age of dissent

all dissents are equal. Certain dissents are more influential than others, "be-com[ing] part of and influenc[ing] the . . . dialogue" (Urofsky 2017, 7). Why are some dissents cited in the future, and others are not? To answer this question, we proposed that well-crafted and attention-grabbing dissents are more likely to be remembered and then cited by future Court majorities. Our focus is on the content of dissenting opinions, and specifically the effect of language on citation behavior.

While the likelihood of any particular past dissent being cited by a future majority in any particular term is overall quite low, we find that a number of stylistic features may significantly increase the likelihood of past dissents becoming part of the future conversation. Future Supreme Court majority opinion writers are more likely to cite past dissents that are written at a higher-grade readability level; rely more on precedent; use a higher percentage of adverbs, adjectives, intensifiers; utilize more distinctive words; and reflect a more narrative style. Taken together, these findings suggest that dissents that strategically craft their arguments to encourage future recall are those more likely to be remembered and then cited by their future colleagues. As discussed in the introduction, dissents are many times written not for one's current colleagues, but rather for external audiences and as pleas for future Courts to reconsider the contemporaneous Court's decision. Dissents that take advantage of writing styles and diction choices that increase their ability to grab attention and spur recall are more likely to see that goal achieved.

Not surprisingly, we also find that ideology matters when it comes to which dissents are influential in the future. Specifically, we find that as a future Court's ideology moves closer to the ideology of the author of the past dissenting opinion, the more likely that future Court will cite the dissent. We also find that newer precedents are more likely to be cited by future majority opinions. Finally, we find that dissents that are more vital, defined as those that have been previously cited positively by prior Supreme Court majority decisions, are more likely to be cited in subsequent terms.

Our results reveal that dissenting authors can strategically use important writing tools to increase the likelihood of future Courts utilizing their arguments. Many of these stylistic features are positively associated with increasing recall, the necessary first step for a past dissent to be remembered and then cited. Our findings also suggest that while dissents may be a way for a justice to simply express discontent with one's colleagues, dissents can also play an important role in the ongoing legal and policy debate. By citing these past dissents, future Courts ensure that these dissents are not only a continuing part of the justices' dialogue but also further embedded into the national legal and policy dialogue. Dissents thus provide a crucial mechanism for enshrining in the public record debates over legal policy and alternative legal arguments. And, much as dissenting coalition members hope they can chip away at the majority during the bargaining phase of a case, so too may dissents serve the long-term purpose of chipping away at the legal policy established by the Court. In our final chapter, we summarize our main findings and explore their implications.

Conclusion

By enabling, indeed compelling, the justices of our Court, through their personally signed majority, dissenting, and concurring opinions, to set forth clear and consistent positions on both sides of the major legal issues of the day, it has kept the Court in the forefront of the intellectual development of the law. In our system, it is not left to the academicians to stimulate and conduct discussion concerning validity of the Court's latest ruling. The Court itself is not just the central organ of legal *judgment;* it is center stage for significant legal *debate.* In our law schools, it is not necessary to assign students the writings of prominent academics in order that they may recognize and reflect upon the principal controversies of legal method or of constitutional law. Those controversies appear in the opposing opinions of the Supreme Court itself, and can be studied from that text.

—Justice Antonin Scalia 1998, 21

T HIS BOOK SEEKS to understand the role of dissents on the US Supreme Court in the national legal and policy dialogue. The justices engage in this discussion publicly through their written opinions. While we know that extensive conversations and discussions occur among the justices during Conference sessions, between chambers, and through the opinion-writing process, our contemporaneous insights come only through the justices' published, final opinions. And, perhaps more importantly, it is only these written opinions that officially contribute to the broader policy and legal debate the justices engage in with other governmental actors and the public.

We propose that the Supreme Court, and really all courts, play a crucial role in the national legal and policy dialogue. The Supreme Court is tasked not only with interpreting the US Constitution and ensuring that all statutes passed by Congress and state legislatures adhere to its parameters, but also

with interpreting federal statutes and regulations. Courts undertake these du-
ties on a daily basis, particularly the job of statutory interpretation. Each time
the Court interprets a statute, or interprets the Constitution, it is adding to
the broader conversation about both law and policy. Especially with respect to
statutory interpretation, this discourse between the judiciary and legislative
and executive branches is dynamic and ongoing, many times spanning decades if not centuries. Each of the Court's entries into this dialogue helps craft
governmental actions and policy itself. In fact, the Court's influence on the legal and policy debate is many times best seen through its statutory decisions,
where the Court's interpretation may directly prompt clarifying legislation
or other legislative, executive, or even public actions. We therefore expand
the definition of the legal and policy dialogue in which the Supreme Court
engages beyond simply a constitutional dialogue to one encompassing the
whole of the Court's work, both constitutional and statutory.

We argue that while the Court's majority opinion reflects the official entry
of the Court into this legal and policy discussion, dissents also play an important and necessary role. Dissents by their very nature proclaim publicly
that important disagreements exist on the Court over the legal question at
hand. Dissents highlight the source of these disagreements, allowing justices
to spell out precisely how and why they believe their colleagues have erred.
They showcase the reality that many legal and policy issues are difficult and
complex, lacking clear answers or easy compromises. And dissents ensure that
the nature and scope of this disagreement is enshrined in the public record,
available to be read by the other justices, lower court judges, members of Congress and the executive branch, state actors and members of agencies, and the
broader public alike. Dissents also push majority coalitions to craft stronger
opinions and to potentially limit the reach of the Court's legal rulings.

But not all dissents are created equal. Some dissents are recorded in the official record but read by very few. Other dissents are widely read, by those on
the Court and beyond. These latter dissents provide important information,
and even guidance, to members of the legislative and executive branches as
well as the public, of how to potentially change the laws in question to successfully achieve certain policy and legal goals. These dissents may similarly
counsel lawyers and outside groups about potential alternative legal arguments and pathways. They can also provide direction to future justices about
arguments to use for revisiting prior Court precedents.

When a dissent is filed, the Court majority helps determine if a dissent's
impact is felt widely or makes barely a ripple. Two potential responses to a

dissent filed in a particular case by the majority exist: to respond to the dissent in the majority opinion, or to ignore it. In some instances, the majority continues the conversation begun in Conference and between chambers by responding to the dissent publicly and formally in the majority opinion. This back-and-forth between the majority and dissenting opinions highlights for the public, and other actors involved in law and policymaking, that this is an important issue of continuing debate and deliberation. And, by including the dissenting arguments in the majority opinion, even if just to show their flaws, those opposing arguments become more firmly embedded in the legal and policy dialogue. In other cases, however, the majority simply ignores the dissent, putting an end to the justices' discussion. What distinguishes those dissents where the majority responds from those where the Court determines the proper response is no response at all?

We theorize that the majority must calculate the costs and benefits of responding as opposed to not responding. By responding, the majority highlights the dissenters' arguments, while ignoring a dissent suggests it offers little of value to the ongoing discussion. Responding instead signals to outside readers of the Court's opinion that the dissent deserves attention. It casts an additional spotlight on the dissent, and ensures that the arguments made by the dissent will be known by everyone who, at the very least, reads the majority opinion.

Thus, why would the majority ever respond? We argue that a contemporaneous Court majority will be more likely to respond when it perceives that the threat posed by the dissent is high, and so the cost of not responding is greater than the cost of responding. We posit that the threat of dissents comes from the dissent's potential ability to weaken the force of the Court's opinion. A dissent by its very definition casts doubt on the correctness of the Court's decision, providing, in the words of Chief Justice William Rehnquist, "an appeal to present and future brethren to see the light" (Rehnquist 1973, 363). We propose that this potential threat will be heightened when the dissent is well crafted, and when it has an increased ability to draw external attention. Well-crafted dissents pose a threat by offering persuasive arguments to others about why the Court's decision is wrong or potentially should be weakened or ignored. Dissents may undermine the strength of Court opinions, potentially undercutting their legitimacy and increasing the possibility of noncompliance. Dissents can provide arguments for lower courts, bureaucratic agencies, or external governmental and public actors to distinguish their actions from, or even wholly ignore, the Court's decision. The more persuasive and well written the dissent, the more the Court may fear such reactions. The threat of external attention works in a similar manner: dissents that draw heightened attention from outside actors, the media, and the public can again serve to undermine the majority decision. A dissent crafted to appeal to external audiences—such as one that overly emphasizes the dangers of the Court's decision in emphatic terms—may in turn spur congressional reactions, public backlash, and other unwanted responses that may undercut the decision and even damage the Court more broadly. We argue that when the Court majority fears these types of responses to the dissent, it will decide to deliberately address the dissent head-on.

Some dissents also play a role in the legal and policy dialogue for many years to come. Perhaps most famously, Justice John Marshall Harlan's sweeping dissent in *Plessy v. Ferguson* (1896), decrying the decision of the Court to condone the doctrine of "separate but equal," was relied on to eventually overturn *Plessy*, and continues to be recalled in discussions of civil rights. Most others, however, will never be read or referred to again. According to Justice Scalia: "Unlike majority opinions, [dissents] need not be read after the date of their issuance. They will not be cited, and will not be remembered, unless some quality of thought or of expression commends them to later generations" (Scalia 1998, 23). We thus ask, why are certain dissents cited by majority opinions in the future while others are not?

We propose that the calculations of a future Court are distinct from those of a contemporaneous Court when determining how to address prior dissents. Here, the Court is deciding whether to positively cite, and even potentially adopt, the arguments posed by the previous dissenters. A future Court has no need to feel threatened by a past dissent. Rather, future Courts potentially pluck prior dissents the Court both recalls and wishes to utilize. Understanding future Court practices is thus about identifying which prior dissents are not only most likely to be remembered and recalled, but also which prior dissents will help the majority opinion writer craft a more persuasive opinion. We argue that the dissents most likely to be used in the future are those that are well written and well grounded in precedent, as well as those that were crafted with an eye toward grabbing external attention. Thus, the same overarching factors that we believe may increase the likelihood that a dissent presents a threat to a contemporaneous Court will also be those that heighten the likelihood of a future Court remembering and then positively citing a prior dissent. These factors function, however, in distinct ways with respect to contemporaneous versus future Courts.

In order to more fully understand the role dissents on United States Supreme Court as well as their role in the broader legal and policy dialogue, we begin with an assessment of when and why dissents occur. In chapter 1 we first trace the evolution of the US Supreme Court from an institution of consensus and acquiescence to one of division. We especially highlight important institutional changes in both formal processes and norms that encouraged, if not enabled, dissent to flourish on the Court. These changes were instituted slowly over time, and many of them unintentionally aided the move toward the modern era of dissensus. From majority opinion authors publicly signing their names to their opinions, to the eventual demise of the Court's mandatory docket, to the formalization of dissent assignments, each subsequent change increased the ease with which justices could express their personal opinions in each case.

We then empirically assess what factors and forces may lead justices in the modern era to dissent in certain cases. Building on our previous work on unanimity at the aggregate level (Corley, Steigerwalt, and Ward 2013), we offer a comprehensive theory of dissenting behavior at the individual level. Our theoretical framework takes into account the multiple and diverse forces that enable individual justices to dissent, including ideological and strategic considerations. Most notably, we extend our previous theory of legal certainty to the question of dissents at the individual level, arguing and finding that when the level of legal certainty is low as to the "correct" legal answer, individual justices are more likely to dissent. But when the level of legal certainty is high, and external signals point toward a single legal answer, individual justices are less likely to dissent.

Chapter 2 continues our overview of the content and character of dissenting behavior by providing the first ever assessment of dissent coalition formation and bargaining. While numerous studies examine majority coalition formation and bargaining, as well as majority opinion author attempts to stave off dissenters, no study has yet examined how dissenters bargain and negotiate amongst themselves. Using the papers of former Justices Lewis Powell and Harry Blackmun, we uncover how justices in the dissent coalition negotiate, bargain, and work together to craft dissents. Not surprisingly, dissenters first try to peel away members of the majority coalition to try to gain the ever-important fifth vote, discussing strategy among themselves. But dissenters then continue their communications to negotiate over the principal dissent opinion content, and to try to prevent additional, separate opinions. We identify four distinct variations of such negotiations, including when justices decline to bargain altogether. And, we reveal how the justices work to craft the strongest possible dissent. Overall, this novel investigation of dissent coalition formation and bargaining helps us to further understand the role of dissent on the US Supreme Court.

Chapters 3 and 4 then turn to the central question of this book: Why do some dissents become embedded in the legal and policy debate while others play little to no role in the development of the law? Chapter 3 examines, once the dissent is entered into the formal record, under what conditions the majority will feel it necessary to respond. We test our theory of dissent threat on all cases containing a dissent decided by the US Supreme Court from 1953 to 2004. We find strong support for our theory: majorities are most likely to feel it necessary to reply to dissents that are well crafted, as well as those that are likely to draw external attention. Specifically, we find that the majority feels most threatened, and thus the greatest need to respond, to dissents that are analytically written and well grounded in precedent. The majority also is more likely to respond to dissents that use attention-grabbing language through the (over)use of adverbs, adjectives, and intensifiers. Finally, Court majorities recognize that dissenting coalitions that are larger and/or more ideologically heterogeneous are more likely to draw outside attention and necessitate a response. We thus find that contemporaneous Courts assess carefully the potential threat posed by dissents, and may decide that the cost of not responding is too high to risk. In those cases, the majority directly addresses the dissent, enmeshing the dissent more formally in the broader legal and policy discussion.

Chapter 4 investigates the role of dissents in the long-term legal and policy dialogue. The majority opinion establishes precedent, but dissents are also a part of the formal record. Justices acknowledge that many times they write these dissents not for the current case, or even the current Court, but as guidance for future Courts. As Chief Justice Charles Hughes explained, "A dissent in a Court of last resort is an appeal . . . to the intelligence of a future day" (1928, 68). Almost a century later, Justice Ruth Bader Ginsburg expressed a similar sentiment: "[Y]ou're writing for a future age, and your hope is that with time the Court will see it the way you do" (Ginsburg 2017). We find that the majority opinions cite dissents that are useful and memorable due to their well-crafted nature and use of attention-grabbing rhetoric. Specifically, future justices are more likely to recall and use prior dissents that are well grounded in precedent and that utilize a more narrative style, thus increasing the likelihood of recall. Future Courts also rely more on past dissents that use a high degree of adverbs, adjectives, and intensifiers, as well as more distinctive, and thus memorable, language. Justices who craft their dissents with an eye to the future, and make use of writing tools that increase recall, are then more likely to see their dissents become a part of the law in the future. Table 5 includes a summary of our findings for each chapter.

What are the implications of our findings? Given the secrecy surrounding the Supreme Court's deliberations and decision-making processes, the opinions the justices write provide insight into their internal discussions and into the reasons behind their votes. The opinions published by the Court become a formal part of the broader legal and policy discourse. Majority opinions clearly have the most impact, as they relate the Court's holding and set legal precedent. Although Justice Oliver Wendall Holmes once described dissents as "useless and undesirable as a rule" (*Northern Securities Co. v. United States* 1904, 400), we argue and find otherwise. Instead, dissents, by highlighting alternative legal arguments, are an integral part of the judicial process. Thus, dissents are neither "useless" nor simply "matters of pique." Rather, dissents both insert valuable information into the dialogue and also shape the majority's contribution to that dialogue. We find that contemporaneous majorities may explicitly and deliberately spend valuable time and effort crafting responses to dissenting arguments. And they are most likely to do so when they determine a dissent poses a threat to the majority's position. The implication is that the majority coalition is concerned with the broader force of its contribution to the legal and policy debate. A majority opinion that is viewed as weak or compromised threatens the Court's ability to have its views heard and respected.

In the *Federalist Papers,* Alexander Hamilton famously sought to soothe concerns about the Supreme Court's power by reminding his readers that the Court lacks the power of the purse and the sword. The lack of taxing or enforcement power means the Supreme Court is dependent on the other branches and external actors viewing the Court's determinations as legitimate and then complying. Thus, while justices from the founding of the Republic have defended their right to express dissenting views, each of these justices also recognizes the potential threat dissents pose. That is why, when those very same justices are in the majority, they both work to fend off dissents as well as to respond forcefully to those dissents that might present a threat to the Court's position and legitimacy.

These findings raise implications for lower federal courts and state courts as well. While we focus in this book on the US Supreme Court, all courts in the United States, and many in other countries as well, must be concerned

TABLE 5. Summary of results in chapters 4 and 5

Variable	Majority Contemporaneously Cites Dissent	Majority Cites Dissent in the Future
Well-Written Dissents		
Reading grade level of dissent	No effect	More likely
Analytically written dissent	More likely	Less likely
Number of precedent (logged)	More likely	More likely
Attention-grabbing Dissents		
Writing style of dissent	More likely	More likely
Negative emotional words	No effect	No effect
Distinctive language	No effect	More likely
Dissent Coalition		
Ideological heterogeneity of dissenters	More likely*	No effect*
Number of dissenters	More likely*	No effect*
Ideological difference between majority and dissent	Less likely	--
Other		
Days until the end of term	More likely	--
Ideological distance between Court median and dissent	--	Less likely
Prop. Of Same Issue Area on Docket	--	More likely
Age of Dissent	--	Less likely
Age-Squared	--	No effect
Age-Cubed	--	No effect
Contemporary Majority Opinion Overruled	--	No effect

*Not included in the same model

with questions of legitimacy and compliance. An area for fruitful future research is therefore the degree to which our theory of threat response helps to explain the likelihood of majority responses to dissents on state high courts, and even the US Courts of Appeals. Future studies may also explore how what a threatening dissent looks like may differ depending on the level of the court, or its structure. And to what degree do similar concerns arise on constitutional courts and high courts in other countries?

Our findings also emphasize the dynamic and continuing nature of the broader legal and policy dialogue. This dialogue does not end simply because a statute is enacted or a judicial decision is rendered. Instead, this dialogue continues through the years as issues, as well as our understanding of the law itself, evolve. Policies are continually implemented, revised, questioned, and reformed, and the courts play a crucial role in interpreting statutes, constitutions, and the legality of governmental actions. Each judicial decision is a new entry into this ongoing interchange and dissents can play a crucial role as well. Justices know that many times their dissents are written for external audiences and future Courts, and so they draft their dissents accordingly. Our findings reveal that future Courts look to prior dissents to give guidance when revisiting legal issues, and that they again look for well-written and memorable dissents. While a relatively small fraction of dissents will be ultimately cited by a future Court, each dissent provides an opportunity for future justices to find direction and support for their views.

This ongoing dialogue is also not confined simply to the constitutional cases that the Court hears. While statutory interpretation cases may not be as newsworthy as civil rights and liberties issues, they are no less important to the development and operation of law in the United States. And it is in these cases that justices many times can exert influence with their dissents well beyond the Court's walls. Our findings therefore also emphasize the necessity of viewing the totality of the Supreme Court's outputs. Examining only constitutional cases obscures the entirety of the of the ways in which the Court routinely influences the development of law and policy in the United States. There is much still to be explored in this vein. Future research could, for example, examine the degree to which legislators and executive agencies use dissents as guides to change policies, statutes, and regulations. Justice Ginsburg rightly took credit for spurring the passage of the Lily Ledbetter Fair Pay Act, but how often does Congress, or specific members of Congress, respond to such judicial entreaties? And how often are those responses successful at changing the law?

Once again, these same implications apply with equal weight, if not more, to other courts within the American judicial system. On the one hand, state courts are increasingly addressing cases based solely on their state constitutions, and not simply the US Constitution. On the other hand, state and federal courts alike overwhelmingly hear statutory and criminal cases where constitutional issues of any level are not implicated. And, particularly for the federal courts, 99 percent of cases filed in federal courts end at the Courts of Appeals. We therefore encourage future research into both the role of these courts in the broader legal and policy debate as well as increased attention to how these courts influence this debate specifically in statutory matters.

A final implication of our findings is the importance of the content of judicial opinions. While clearly the substantive content of the justices' legal arguments matter, we also find that *how* that content is expressed matters greatly. Justices take care when drafting opinions not simply to determine the outlines of their arguments, but also how to best present those arguments. The choice to use a more formal, analytical style as opposed to a more narrative style may impact how an opinion is received as well as its likelihood of recall. Similarly, writing guides emphasize simplicity and toned-down language. But "bad" writing, such as the use of adverbs, adjectives, and intensifiers, may serve the justices' broader goals. Distinctive language, or overly emotional language, may likewise offer efficient tools to convey the full extent of a justice's dismay to those outside the Court.

What else do these results suggest for future research? We can think of a number of additional avenues for further exploration. One obvious approach would be to examine the role dissents play when it comes to other audiences, such as Congress, the public, or the media. We specifically focus in this book on the discussion that takes place *within* the Supreme Court. However, previous research demonstrates that dissents may have various external effects. Amanda C. Bryan and Eve M. Ringsmuth (2016) find that Supreme Court decisions with negative dissents attract more media coverage. James R. Zink, James F. Spriggs II, and John T. Scott (2009) find that the public is less likely to agree with and accept non-unanimous decisions. Conversely, Michael F. Salamone (2014, 322) finds that the public is more willing to accept a decision involving a low-salience issue when there is a dissent, perhaps because dissents can be taken as evidence of a fair, deliberative process. How do these external audiences react to well-crafted and attention-grabbing dissents? Are these types of dissents more likely to garner media attention, or to aid either compliance levels or public approval? Are these dissents, and especially those that use attention-grabbing, emotional language, more likely to capture the attention of members of Congress and spur legislative change, as Walter F. Murphy (1964) posited? Similarly, to what degree have dissents aided outside interest groups and litigants in forming alternative legal and political strategies?

Supreme Court decisions are obviously directed first and foremost at other judges because they provide guidance on similar cases. While our assessment focuses on the dialogue between the justices, other judges in the American judiciary also play a role, both responding to Supreme Court decisions and issuing their own decisions. How do dissents influence lower court reactions to Supreme Court precedents? Do they affect the extent to which lower federal courts and state courts, those tasked with the responsibility of interpreting and applying binding precedent, comply with Supreme Court precedents? For example, do lower courts, especially those ideologically distant from the Supreme Court majority opinion, rely on dissents to evade or even defy precedent? Are well-crafted and attention-grabbing dissents more likely to be referenced by these courts, or do judges on these courts respond to different dissent writing characteristics than justices on the Supreme Court?

Finally, how should we understand the role of dissents on courts where their occurrence is not as common, such as the federal Courts of Appeals? For example, only 9.5 percent of cases included in the Courts of Appeals Database decided during the 1960 to 1996 period contained a dissenting opinion (Hettinger, Lindquist, and Martinek 2006, 47). When a dissent does emerge, are Courts of Appeals more or less likely to engage with dissents? While we find that only a fraction of dissents overall are discussed by Supreme Court majorities, does the rarity of dissent potentially lead to an increased amount of attention given to such dissents when they do occur? Further, do different dissent characteristics influence the extent to which Courts of Appeals majority opinions cite dissents? Put another way, does our theory of threat response help to explain the dialogue that occurs on the federal appeals courts, or do dissents play a different role at that level of the federal judicial hierarchy? To what degree do appeals courts reference prior dissenting opinions? And, for what uses? Again, does the rarity of dissent on these courts overall lead to an increased likelihood that these dissents are utilized in the future to revisit precedents on the Courts of Appeals?

Overall, our results showcase the complexity of understanding the broader legal and policy dialogue, which encompasses all the branches of government. The US Supreme Court is an important player in this ongoing debate, and our findings reveal how the Court's contributions do not always constitute a monolithic entity. Rather, the Court in each case might make multiple entries into the conversation. We must therefore understand how each of these entries comes to fruition, and also how each entry influences the other, in order to fully appreciate the role the Court has in influencing this dialogue, and policy itself, now and in the future. It is only by understanding the role dissents play on the Court, and how these dissents may also influence the Court's contributions to the broader legal and policy discussions, that we can truly understand the role of the US Supreme Court in the national policy-making process.

NOTES

Introduction

1. Although the Court upheld the act under both the Equal Protection Clause and the Commerce Clause, we focus on the Court's analysis of the Equal Protection Clause claims.

2. We note that many in the field of political communication use the term "dialogue" to mean a desire between participants to achieve mutual understanding and tolerance, while the term "deliberation" reflects discussions that have the goal of determining issue positions or making policy decisions (see, e.g., Cramer Walsh 2007; Thompson 2008). We use the term "dialogue" throughout this book, even as we at times are focusing on the process of participants determining their issue positions, to reflect the broad nature of the conversation the justices are engaged in and the fact that the dialogue does not end simply because a decision of the Court's majority is rendered. Rather, the dialogue is dynamic and ongoing, more reflective of a continuing conversation than a process conceived to reach a defined end.

3. Lewis F. Powell Jr. to Phil Jordan, January 12, 1976, Powell Papers, Box 173.

4. William Brennan to the Conference, February 11, 1976, Powell Papers, Box 173.

5. Lewis F. Powell Jr. to the Conference, February 12, 1976, Powell Papers, Box 173.

6. Lewis F. Powell Jr. handwritten note on Brennan's draft opinion, February 13, 1976, Powell Papers, Box 173.

7. Lewis F. Powell Jr. to Michael W. Mosman, January 23, 1986, Powell Papers, Box 269.

8. Lewis F. Powell Jr. to Anne M. Coughlin, April 24, 1986, Powell Papers, Box 269.

1. Dissenting Behavior on the US Supreme Court

1. As an associate justice under Chief Justice Edward White, Hughes voted in dissent in only 2.3 percent (34/1,453) of the cases he decided and issued dissenting opinions less than 1 percent (7/1,453) of the time. As chief justice, Hughes increased those totals, voting in dissent 3.2 percent (59/1,843) of the time and issuing dissenting opinions in 1.5 percent of cases (28/1,843).

2. Silent acquiescence still continued throughout the Burger Court, but very rarely and mostly in comparatively unimportant cases (Goelzhauser 2015).

3. Mary Becker to Lewis F. Powell Jr., April 29, 1982, Powell Papers, Box 233.

4. Lewis F. Powell Jr. to William J. Brennan Jr., December 13, 1985, Powell Papers, Box 269.

5. William J. Brennan Jr. to Byron White, January 27, 1977, White Papers, Box 388.

6. William J. Brennan Jr. to Thurgood Marshall, May 4, 1987, Brennan Papers, Box 742.

7. Harry A. Blackmun to Sandra Day O'Connor, January 16, 1984, Blackmun Papers.

8. Sandra Day O'Connor to Harry A. Blackmun, January 19, 1984, Blackmun Papers.

9. Harry A. Blackmun to Sandra Day O'Connor, January 19, 1984, Blackmun Papers.

10. Sandra Day O'Connor to Harry A. Blackmun, January 23, 1984, Blackmun Papers.

11. Potter Stewart to Warren E. Burger, April 6, 1981, Powell Papers, Box 224.

12. William H. Rehnquist to William J. Brennan Jr., May 6, 1986, Blackmun Papers, Box 456.

13. Lewis F. Powell Jr. to Dick Fallon, April 22, 1982, Powell Papers, Box 232.

14. Sandra Day O'Connor to Lewis F. Powell Jr., June 9, 1982, Powell Papers, Box 232.

15. Epstein, Landes, and Posner (2011) use the term "dissent aversion," which they argue sometimes causes a justice not to dissent even when that justice disagrees with the majority opinion.

16. Because of our hypothesis regarding level of legal certainty (and how that is measured, which we explain below), appeals cases and cases appealed from state courts were necessarily excluded from the analysis.

17. We substituted cases that are listed as landmark cases by *Congressional Quarterly* as our measure for politically salient cases instead of those that appeared on the front page of the *New York Times* the day after the decision is announced, and the results are substantially similar.

18. We also tested for the possibility of a dampening effect of cotenure on the ideological disagreement between justices by interacting the cotenure variable with the ideological difference between the justice and the majority opinion author. However, there was no interaction effect between the two variables.

2. Endeavoring to Accommodate

1. See Powell Papers, Box 231.

2. Lewis F. Powell Jr. to Warren E. Burger, April 29, 1982, Powell Papers, Box 229.

3. Lewis F. Powell Jr. to Harry A. Blackmun, January 28, 1977, Powell Papers, Box 184.

4. Lewis F. Powell Jr. to Warren E. Burger, April 27, 1981, Powell Papers, Box 218.

5. David Patterson to Harry A. Blackmun, May 27, 1976, Blackmun Papers, Box 227.

6. David Patterson to Harry A. Blackmun, June 3, 1976, Blackmun Papers, Box 227.

7. David Patterson to Harry A. Blackmun, June 17, 1976, Blackmun Papers, Box 227.

8. William H. Rehnquist to Thurgood Marshall, May 14, 1982, Powell Papers, Box 232.

9. Lewis F. Powell Jr. to Thurgood Marshall, May 14, 1982, Powell Papers, Box 232

10. Sandra Day O'Connor to Thurgood Marshall, May 19, 1982, Powell Papers, Box 232

11. Byron White to Thurgood Marshall, May 17, 1982, Powell Papers, Box 232

12. Lewis F. Powell Jr. to David Levi, June 10, 1982, Powell Papers, Box 232

13. Lewis F. Powell Jr. to Warren E. Burger, May 27, 1976, Powell Papers, Box 177.

14. Lewis F. Powell Jr. to Warren E. Burger, May 27, 1976, Powell Papers, Box 177.

15. Dick Fallon to Lewis F. Powell Jr., March 28, 1982, Powell Papers, Box 231.

16. William J. Brennan to Lewis F. Powell Jr., May 10, 1982, Powell Papers, Box 231.

17. Lewis F. Powell Jr. to William J. Brennan, May 17, 1982, Powell Papers, Box 231.

18. William J. Brennan to Lewis F. Powell Jr., May 19, 1982, Powell Papers, Box 231.

19. Lewis F. Powell Jr. to Sandra Day O'Connor, March 4, 1986, Powell Papers, Box 269.

20. Sandra Day O'Connor to Lewis F. Powell Jr., March 7, 1986, Powell Papers, Box 269.

21. Antonin Scalia to the Conference, May 19, 1987, Powell Papers, Box 282.

22. Sandra Day O'Connor to Byron R. White, May 20, 1987, Powell Papers, Box 282.

23. Warren Burger to Byron R. White, June 30, 1976, Powell Papers, Box 176.

24. John Wiley to Lewis F. Powell Jr., December 28, 1981, Powell Papers, Box 229.

25. Lewis F. Powell Jr. to Sandra Day O'Connor, June 22, 1982, Powell Papers, Box 235.

26. Sandra Day O'Connor to Lewis F. Powell Jr., June 23, 1982, Powell Papers, Box 235.

27. Lewis F. Powell Jr. handwritten note on O'Connor's draft opinion, June 29, 1982, Powell Papers, Box 235.

28. Warren E. Burger to Lewis F. Powell Jr., June 17, 1982, Powell Papers, Box 233.

29. Lewis F. Powell Jr. to Harry A. Blackmun, June 22, 1981, Powell Papers, Box 224.

30. Lewis F. Powell Jr. to the Conference, March 3, 1977, Powell Papers, Box 185.

31. Lewis F. Powell Jr. to the Conference, March 3, 1977, Powell Papers, Box 185.

32. Warren E. Burger to Potter Stewart, April 4, 1981, Powell Papers, Box 224.

33. Potter Stewart to Warren E. Burger, April 6, 1981, Powell Papers, Box 224.

34. Warren E. Burger to William Rehnquist, April 6, 1981, Powell Papers, Box 224.

35. Lewis F. Powell Jr. to Michael W. Mosman, January 23, 1986, Powell Papers, Box 269.

36. Lewis F. Powell Jr. to Antonin Scalia, January 7, 1987, Powell Papers, Box 279.

37. Antonin Scalia to Lewis F. Powell Jr., January 8, 1987, Powell Papers, Box 279.

38. Lewis F. Powell Jr. to Leslie S. Gielow, April 29, 1987, Powell Papers, Box 285.

39. Lewis F. Powell Jr. to Leslie S. Gielow, June 16, 1987, Powell Papers, Box 285.

40. Lewis F. Powell Jr. to Harry A. Blackmun, June 23, 1987, Powell Papers, Box 285.

41. William Rehnquist to Lewis F. Powell Jr., February 18, 1987, Powell Papers, Box 280.

42. Mary Becker to Lewis F. Powell Jr., June 12, 1982, Powell Papers, Box 233.

43. Lewis F. Powell Jr., to Mary Becker, June 14, 1982, Powell Papers, Box 233.

44. Lewis F. Powell Jr. handwritten note on Stewart's draft opinion, May 18, 1976, Powell Papers, Box 178.

45. Lewis F. Powell Jr. handwritten note on Rehnquist's draft opinion, December 17, 1985, Powell Papers, Box 269.

46. William Rehnquist to Lewis F. Powell Jr., April 29, 1981, Powell Papers, Box 223.

47. Warren E. Burger to Lewis F. Powell Jr., undated, Powell Papers, Box 223.

48. Greg Morgan to Lewis F. Powell Jr., May 1, 1981, Powell Papers, Box 223.

49. Lewis F. Powell Jr. to Greg Morgan, May 1, 1981, Powell Papers, Box 223.

50. Lewis F. Powell, Jr. handwritten note on Stewart's draft opinion, March 25, 1981, Powell Papers, Box 224.

51. Paul Smith to Lewis F. Powell Jr., May 27, 1981, Powell Papers, Box 224.

52. Lewis F. Powell Jr. to Paul Smith, May 27, 1981, Powell Papers, Box 224.

53. Paul Smith to Lewis F. Powell Jr., June 16, 1981, Powell Papers, Box 224.

54. Lewis F. Powell Jr. to Warren E. Burger, June 16, 1981, Powell Papers, Box 224.

55. Lewis F. Powell Jr. to Harry A. Blackmun, April 17, 1986, Powell Papers, Box 273.

56. Harry A. Blackmun to Lewis F. Powell Jr., April 18, 1986, Powell Papers, Box 273.

57. Lewis F. Powell Jr. handwritten note on Blackmun's draft, April 18, 1986, Powell Papers, Box 273.

58. Antonin Scalia to Lewis F. Powell Jr., June 1, 1987, Powell Papers, Box 281.

59. Sandra Day O'Connor to Lewis F. Powell Jr., June 10, 1987, Powell Papers, Box 281.

60. Lewis F. Powell Jr. to Sandra Day O'Connor, June 11, 1987, Powell Papers, Box 281.

61. Warren E. Burger to Lewis F. Powell Jr., June 22, 1982, Powell Papers, Box 235.

62. Lewis F. Powell Jr. to Warren E. Burger, June 22, 1982, Powell Papers, Box 235.

63. Harry A. Blackmun to Lewis F. Powell Jr., February 22, 1987, Powell Papers, Box 280.

64. John Paul Stevens to William Rehnquist, June 3, 1976, Blackmun Papers, Box 233.
65. William Rehnquist to Byron White, March 30, 1977, Blackmun Papers, Box 246.
66. Harry A. Blackmun to Byron White, April 6, 1977, Blackmun Papers, Box 246.
67. William Rehnquist to Byron White, April 6, 1977, Blackmun Papers, Box 246.
68. Lewis F Powell Jr. to Potter Stewart, Byron White, and William Rehnquist, June 22, 1976, Powell Papers, Box 176.
69. Ronald Mann to Lewis F. Powell Jr., December 4, 1986, Powell Papers, Box 279.
70. Lewis F. Powell Jr. to Antonin Scalia, February 13, 1987, Powell Papers, Box 279.
71. Antonin Scalia to Lewis F. Powell Jr., February 18, 1987, Powell Papers, Box 279.
72. Lewis F. Powell Jr. to John Paul Stevens, October 14, 1981, Powell Papers, Box 229.
73. John Paul Stevens to Lewis F. Powell Jr., October 15, 1981, Powell Papers, Box 229.
74. Potter Stewart to Lewis F. Powell Jr., February 3, 1981, Powell Papers, Box 220.
75. Paul Cane to Lewis F. Powell Jr., February 3, 1981, Powell Papers, Box 220.
76. Lewis F. Powell Jr. to Paul Cane, February 3, 1981, Powell Papers, Box 220.
77. Paul Cane to Lewis F. Powell Jr., February 6, 1981, Powell Papers, Box 220.
78. Lewis F. Powell Jr. to Potter Stewart, February 12, 1981, Powell Papers, Box 220.
79. Warren E. Burger to the Conference, May 31, 1977, Powell Papers, Box 187.
80. Lewis F. Powell Jr. handwritten note on Burger's opinion draft, January 25, 1986, Powell Papers, Box 268.
81. Lewis F. Powell Jr. handwritten note on White's draft opinion, June 5, 1986, Powell Papers, Box 272.
82. Sandra Day O'Connor to Warren E. Burger, December 3, 1981, Powell Papers, Box 228.
83. Lewis F. Powell Jr. to Sandra Day O'Connor, December 15, 1981, Powell Papers, Box 228.
84. Greg Morgan to Lewis F. Powell Jr., April 28, 1981, Powell Papers, Box 225.
85. Lewis F. Powell Jr. to Greg Morgan, May 20, 1981, Powell Papers, Box 225.
86. Lewis F. Powell Jr. to David Levi, June 8, 1982, Powell Papers, Box 229.
87. Lewis F. Powell Jr. to Sandra Day O'Connor, February 18, 1987, Powell Papers, Box 279.
88. John Paul Stevens to Potter Stewart, March 18, 1976, Blackmun Papers, Box 218.

3. Intra-Court Dialogue

1. We also substituted alternative readability measures (e.g., Gunning Fog, Coleman Liau, and Linsear Write) in the model and the results are substantially similar.
2. We use the 2015 LIWC dictionary.
3. As with any linguistic software program, LIWC has its limitations. Given that LIWC is a dictionary-based program, it does not capture all nuances of communication — it ignores context, irony, and sarcasm. Additionally, judicial opinions are a unique form of written language, written with a specific format and structure by people with specialized training; however, this does not mean the program cannot be used on legal texts. Numerous prior studies apply LIWC to judicial texts. These scholars have considered categories such as emotional language (Black et al. 2016; Bryan and Ringsmuth 2016; Hume 2019; Dietrich, Enos, and Sen 2019; Zilis and Wed-

king 2020), certainty (Corley and Wedeking 2014), risk focus (Ballingrud 2020), authentic language (Romano and Curry 2019), analytic language (Romano and Curry 2019), and, combining several categories, cognitive complexity (Owens and Wedeking 2011; Collins, Corley, and Hamner 2015; Budziak, Hitt, and Lempert 2019; Romano and Curry 2019; Boston 2020). Despite any limitations, we think it worthwhile to mention that there is no current program available that is able to capture *all* of the relevant elements of judicial opinions. LIWC thus offers a comprehensive text analysis program that has been used successfully, including in numerous studies of judicial opinion content.

4. We thank James F. Spriggs II for providing the raw data.

5. Using *Black's Law Dictionary* (2014), we removed the following common legal terms from the intensifier list: very heavy work, clearly erroneous, wholly and permanently disabled, wholly dependent, wholly destroyed, wholly disabled, completely integrated contract, and highly prudent person.

6. We use June 30, the typical end-of-term date rather than the actual date the term ends, given that the justices themselves will not necessarily know, when they are drafting and revising opinions, what the actual end-of-term date will be. Maltzman, Spriggs, and Wahlbeck (2000) similarly use July 1 rather than the actual date the term ends when analyzing opinion writing.

7. We exclude partial dissents and dissents that contain fewer than 100 words.

8. We acknowledge that a more nuanced measure would be preferable, such as the number of words the majority adds to the opinion directly addressing the dissent. However, there are two related issues with such a measure. One, it is not always clear from the published majority opinion when the majority is directly responding to the dissent (or, more specifically, when the majority has stopped addressing the dissent and is continuing with its original argument). Two, the only way to accurately capture what the majority added to its opinion in response to a circulated dissent would be to examine the draft opinions of every majority opinion and compare the language, and every majority opinion draft from 1953 to 2004 is not currently available.

9. Lewis F. Powell Jr. to Cammie R. Robinson, David A. Charny, Joseph E. Neuhaus, and Robert M. Couch, June 23, 1984, Powell Papers, Box 130b.

4. Judicial Conversations through Time

1. We thank Rachael Hinkle and Michael Nelson for providing the replication data (see Hinkle and Nelson 2018).

REFERENCES

Court Cases

Aldinger v. Howard, 427 U.S. 1 (1976).

Arizona v. Hicks, 480 U.S. 321 (1987).

Arkansas Louisiana Gas Co. v. Hall, 453 U.S. 571 (1981).

Bender v. Williamsport Area School District, 475 U.S. 534 (1986).

Bowers v. Hardwick, 478 U.S. 186 (1986).

Briscoe v. Bank of Commonwealth of Kentucky, 36 U.S. 257 (1837).

Brown v. Barry, 3 U.S. (3 Dall.) 365 (1797).

Brown v. Board of Education, 347 U.S. 483 (1954).

Buffalo Forge Co. v. United States Steelworkers, 428 U.S. 397 (1976).

Bullington v. Missouri, 451 U.S. 430 (1981).

Burger v. Kemp, 483 U.S. 776 (1987).

Burnet v. Coronado Oil & Gas Co., 285 U.S. 393 (1932).

California Coastal Commission v. Granite Rock Co., 480 U.S. 572 (1987).

California v. Rooney, 483 U.S. 307 (1987).

Charles D. Bonanno Linen Service, Inc. v. NLRB, 454 U.S. 404 (1982).

Chisholm v. Georgia, 2 U.S. (2 Dall.) 419 (1793).

City of Eastlake v. Forest City Enterprises, 426 U.S. 668 (1976).

Civil Rights Cases, 109 U.S. 3 (1883).

Clayton v. Automobile Workers, 451 U.S. 679 (1981).

Colorado River Water Conservation District v. United States, 424 U.S. 800 (1976).

Commonwealth Edison v. Montana, 453 U.S. 609 (1981).

Connecticut v. Teal, 457 U.S. 440 (1982).

Cory v. White, 457 U.S. 85 (1982).

County of Washington, Oregon v. Gunther, 452 U.S. 161 (1981).

Crawford Fitting Co. v. J. T. Gibbons, 482 U.S. 437 (1987).

Desist v. United States, 394 U.S. 244 (1969).

Dickerson v. United States, 530 U.S. 428 (2000).

Dow Chemical Co. v. United States, 476 U.S. 227 (1986).

Doyle v. Ohio, 426 U.S. 610 (1976).

Dred Scott v. Sandford, 60 U.S. (19 How.) 393 (1857).

Enmund v. Florida, 458 U.S. 782 (1982).

Ex parte Bollman, 8 U.S. (4 Cranch) 75 (1807).

Federal Power Commissioner v. Hope Natural Gas Co., 320 U.S. 591 (1944).

Fontain v. Ravenel, 58 U.S. (17 How.) 369 (1854).

Foremost Insurance Co. v. Richardson, 457 U.S. 668 (1982).

Franks v. Bowman, 424 U.S. 747 (1976).

Georgia v. Brailsford, 2 U.S. (2 Dall.) 415 (1793).

Goodman v. Lukens Steel Co., 482 U.S. 656 (1987).

Griffith v. Kentucky, 479 U.S. 314 (1987).

Hamdi v. Rumsfeld, 542 U.S. 547 (2004).
Hepburn v. Griswold, 75 U.S. (8 Wall.) 603 (1870).
Humphrey's Executor v. United Sates, 295 U.S. 602 (1935).
Ingraham v. Wright, 430 U.S. 651 (1977).
International Union v. Brock, 477 U.S. 274 (1986).
Interstate Commerce Commission v. American Trucking Association, 467 U.S. 354 (1984).
Jacksonville Bulk Terminals v. Longshoremen, 457 U.S. 702 (1982).
Japan Whaling Assn. v. American Cetacean Society, 478 U.S. 221 (1986).
Jones v. City of Opelika, 316 U.S. 584 (1942).
King v. Burwell, 576 U.S. 473 (2015).
Lawrence Cantor, dba Selden Drugs Co. v. The Detroit Edison Co., 428 U.S. 579 (1976).
Lawrence v. Texas, 539 U.S. 558 (2003).
Ledbetter v. Goodyear Tire& Rubber Co., 550 U.S. 618 (2007).
Lee v. Illinois, 476 U.S. 530 (1986).
Legal Tender Cases, 79 U.S. (12 Wall.) 457 (1871).
Linkletter v. Walker, 381 U.S. 618 (1965).
Lugar v. Edmondson Oil Co., 457 U.S. 922 (1982).
Magnolia Petroleum Co. v. Hunt, 320 U.S. 430 (1943).
Mapp v. Ohio, 367 U.S. 643 (1961).
Martin v. Ohio, 480 U.S. 228 (1987).
Martin v. Struthers, 319 U.S. 141 (1943).
Mason v. Haile, 25 U.S. (12 Wheat.) 370 (1827).
Metropolitan Life Insurance Co. v. Ward, 479 U.S. 869 (1985).
Minersville School District v. Gobitis, 310 U.S. 586 (1940).
Minnesota v. Clover Leaf Creamery Co., 449 U.S. 456 (1981).
Miranda v. Arizona, 384 U.S. 436 (1966).
Mississippi University for Women v. Hogan, 458 U.S. 718 (1982).
Monroe v. Standard Oil Co., 452 U.S. 549 (1981).
Myers v. United States, 272 U.S. 52 (1926).
Nebbia v. New York, 291 U.S. 502 (1934).
New York v. Quarles, 467 U.S. 649 (1984).
NLRB v. Allis-Chalmers Mfg. Co., 388 U.S. 175 (1967).
Northern Securities. Co. v. United States, 193 U.S. 197 (1904).
North Haven Board of Education v. Bell, 456 U.S. 512 (1982).
Nyquist v. Mauclet, 432 U.S. 1 (1977).
Patsy v. Board of Regents, 457 U.S. 496 (1982).
Patterson v. New York, 432 U.S. 197 (1977).
Pembaur v. City of Cincinnati, 475 U.S. 469 (1986).
Pennhurst v. Halderman, 465 U.S. 89 (1984).
Plessy v. Ferguson, 163 U.S. 537 (1896).
The Propeller Monticello v. Mollison, 58 U.S. (17 How.) 152 (1854).
Pulley v. Harris, 465 U.S. 37 (1984).
Ribnik v. McBride, 277 U. S. 350 (1928).

Ridgway v. Ridgway, 454 U.S. 46 (1981).
Seminole Tribe v. Florida, 517 U.S. 44 (1996).
Shea v. Louisiana, 470 U.S. 51 (1985).
Shelby County v. Holder, 570 U.S. 529 (2013).
Sierra Club v. Morton, 405 U.S. 727 (1972).
Singleton v. Wulff, 428 U.S. 106 (1976).
Smoot Sand & Gravel Corp. v. Washington Airport, Inc., 283 U.S. 348 (1931).
Southern Pacific Co. v. Jensen, 244 U.S. 205 (1917).
Steadman v. SEC, 450 U.S. 91 (1981).
Sykes v. Chadwick, 85 U.S. (18 Wall.) 141 (1873).
Talbot v. Seeman, 5 U.S. (Cranch 1) 1 (1801).
Texaco v. Short, 454 U.S. 516 (1982).
Transcontinental Gas Pipe Line Co. v. State Oil and Gas Board of Mississippi, 474 U.S. 409 (1986).
Tyson & Brother v. Banton, 273 U.S. 418 (1927).
United States v. Jacobsen, 466 U.S. 109 (1984).
United States v. Johnson, 457 U.S. 537 (1982).
United States v. Virginia, 518 U.S. 515 (1996).
Vendo Co. v. Lektro-Vend Corp., 433 U.S. 623 (1977).
West Virginia State Board of Education v. Barnette, 319 U.S. 624 (1943).
West Virginia University Hospitals v. Casey, 499 U.S. 83 (1991).
Williams v. Commissioner of Internal Revenue, 429 U.S. 569 (1977).
Winans v. New York & Erie Railroad Co., 62 U.S. 21 (How. 88) 88 (1858).
Wooley v. Maynard, 430 U.S. 705 (1977).
Young v. United States ex rel. Vuitton et Fils, 481 U.S. 787 (1987).

Secondary Sources

Baird, Vanessa A. 2004. "The Effect of Politically Salient Decisions on the US Supreme Court's Agenda." *Journal of Politics* 66, no. 3: 755–72.

Baird, Vanessa A., and Tonja Jacobi. 2009. "How the Dissent Becomes the Majority: Using Federalism to Transform Coalitions in the U.S. Supreme Court." *Duke Law Journal* 59: 183–238.

Ballingrud, Gordon. 2020. "Ideology and Risk Focus: Conservatism and Opinion-Writing in the U.S. Supreme Court." *Social Science Quarterly* 102, no. 1: 281–300.

Barnes, Jeb, and Mark C. Miller. 2004. "Putting the Pieces Together: American Lawmaking from an Interbranch Perspective." In *Making Policy, Making Law: An Interbranch Perspective*, ed. Mark C. Miller and Jeb Barnes, 3–12. Washington, DC: Georgetown University Press.

Bartels, Brandon. 2011. "Choices in Context: How Case-Level Factors Shape the Magnitude of Ideological Voting on the U.S. Supreme Court." *American Politics Research* 39: 142–75.

Baum, Lawrence. 1997. *The Puzzle of Judicial Behavior*. Ann Arbor: University of Michigan Press.

Bennett, Thomas B., Barry Friedman, Andrew D. Martin, and Susan Navarro Smelcer. 2018. "Divide and Concur: Separate Opinions and Legal Change." *Cornell Law Review* 103: 817–77.

Benson, Robert W., and Joan B. Kessler. 1987. "Legalese v. Plain English: An Empirical Study of Persuasion and Credibility in Appellate Brief Writing." *Loyola Los Angeles Law Review* 20: 301.

Black, Ryan C., Ryan J. Owens, Justin Wedeking, and Patrick C. Wohlfarth. 2016. *U.S. Supreme Court and Their Audiences.* New York: Cambridge University Press.

Black, Ryan C., and James F. Spriggs II. 2013. "The Citation and Depreciation of U.S. Supreme Court Precedent." *Journal of Empirical Legal Studies* 10: 325–58.

Black's Law Dictionary. 2014. Eagan, MN: Thomson West.

Blackstone, Bethany. 2013. "An Analysis of Policy-Based Congressional Responses to the U.S. Supreme Court's Constitutional Decisions." *Law & Society Review* 47, no. 1: 199–228.

Blaustein, Albert P., and Roy M. Mersky. 1978. *The First One Hundred Justices: Statistical Studies on the Supreme Court of the United States.* Hamden, CT: Archon Books.

Boston, Joshua. 2020. "Strategic Opinion Language on the US Courts of Appeals." *Journal of Law & Courts* 8: 1–26.

Brennan, William J. 1959. Address to the Student Legal Forum, Charlottesville, VA, February 17, 1959.

Brennan, William J., Jr. 1986. "In Defense of Dissents." *Hastings Law Journal* 37: 427–38.

Brenner, Saul, and Harold J. Spaeth. 1988. "Ideological Position as a Variable in the Authoring of Dissenting Opinions on the Warren and Burger Courts." *American Politics Quarterly* 16: 317–28.

———. 1995. *Stare Indecisis: The Alteration of Precedent on the Supreme Court, 1946–1992.* New York: Cambridge University Press.

Brenner, Saul, Harold J. Spaeth, and Timothy M. Hagle. 1990. "Increasing the Size of Minimum Winning Original Coalitions on the Warren Court." *Polity* 23, no. 2: 309–18.

Bryan, Amanda C., and Eve M. Ringsmuth. 2016. "Jeremiad or Weapon of Words? The Power of Emotive Language in Supreme Court Opinions." *Journal of Law and Courts* 4: 159–85.

Budziak, Jeffrey, Matthew P. Hitt, and Daniel Lempert. 2019. "Determinants of Writing Style on the United States Circuit Courts." *Journal of Law and Courts* 7, no. 1: 1–28.

Burgess, Susan. 1992. *Contest for Constitutional Authority: The Abortion and War Powers Debates.* Lawrence: University Press of Kansas.

Caldeira, Gregory A., and Christopher J. W. Zorn. 1998. "Of Time and Consensual Norms in the Supreme Court." *American Journal of Political Science* 42: 874–902.

Canon, Bradley C., and Charles A. Johnson. 1999. *Judicial Policies: Implementation and Impact.* 2nd ed. Washington, DC: CQ Press.

Carter, David B., and Curtis S. Signorino. 2010. "Back to the Future: Modeling Time Dependence in Binary Data." *Political Analysis* 18, no. 3: 271–92.

Civettini, Andrew J. W., and David P. Redlawsk. 2009. "Voters, Emotions, and Memory." *Political Psychology* 30: 125–51.

Collins, Paul M., Jr. 2008. "Amici Curiae and Dissensus on the United States Supreme Court." *Journal of Empirical Legal Studies* 5: 143–70.

———. 2011. "Cognitive Dissonance on the U.S. Supreme Court." *Political Research Quarterly* 64: 362–76.

Collins, Paul M., Jr., Pamela C. Corley, and Jesse Hamner. 2015. "The Influence of Amicus Curiae Briefs on the U.S. Supreme Court." *Law & Society Review* 49, no. 4: 917–44.

Cook, Beverly Blair. 1995. "Justice Brennan and the Institutionalization of Dissent Assignment." *Judicature* 79: 17–23.

Corley, Pamela C. 2010. *Concurring Opinion Writing on the U.S. Supreme Court.* Albany: State University of New York Press.

Corley, Pamela C., Paul M. Collins Jr., and Bryan Calvin. 2011. "Lower Court Influence on U.S. Supreme Court Opinion Content." *Journal of Politics* 73, no. 1: 31–44.

Corley, Pamela C., Amy Steigerwalt, and Artemus Ward. 2013. *The Puzzle of Unanimity: Consensus on the United States Supreme Court.* Stanford, CA: Stanford University Press.

Corley, Pamela C., and Artemus Ward. 2020. "Intra-Court Dialogue: The Impact of U.S. Supreme Court Dissents." *Journal of Law and Courts* 8, no. 1: 27–50.

Corley, Pamela C., and Justin Wedeking. 2014. "The (Dis)Advantage of Certainty: The Importance of Certainty in Language." *Law & Society Review* 48: 35–62.

Coscia, Michele. 2014. "Average Is Boring: How Similarity Kills a Meme's Success." *Scientific Reports* 4: 6744.

Cramer Walsh, K. 2007. *Talking About Race: Community Dialogues and the Politics of Difference.* Chicago: University of Chicago Press.

Cross, Frank B., and Stefanie A. Lindquist. 2006. "Doctrinal and Strategic Influences of the Chief Justice." *University of Pennsylvania Law Review* 154: 1665–707.

Currie, David P. 1985. *The Constitution in the Supreme Court: The First Hundred Years, 1789–1888.* Chicago: University of Chicago Press.

Dahl, Robert A. 1957. "Decision-Making in a Democracy: The Supreme Court as a National Policy-Maker." *Journal of Public Law* 6, no. 2: 279–95.

Danescu-Niculescu-Mizil, Christian, Justin Cheng, Jon Kleinberg, and Lillian Lee. 2012. "You Had Me at Hello: How Phrasing Affects Memorability." *ACL '12 Proceedings of the 50th Annual Meeting of the Association for Computational Linguistics: Long Papers* 1: 892–901.

D'Argembeau, Arnaud, and Martial Van der Linden. 2005. "Influence of Emotion on Memory for Temporal Information." *Emotion* 5: 503–7.

Devins, Neal. 1996. *Shaping Constitutional Values: Elected Government, the Supreme Court, and the Abortion Debate.* Baltimore: Johns Hopkins University Press.

Devins, Neal, and Lawrence Baum. 2016. "Split Definitive: How Party Polarization Turned the Supreme Court into a Partisan Court." *Supreme Court Review* 2016: 301–65.

Dietrich, Bryce J., Ryan D. Enos, and Maya Sen. 2019. "Emotional Arousal Predicts Voting on the U.S. Supreme Court." *Political Analysis* 27, no. 2: 237–43.

Dolbeare, Kenneth M., and Phillip E. Hammond. 1971. *The School Prayer Decisions: From Court Policy to Local Practice.* Chicago: University of Chicago Press.

Douglas, William O. 1948. "Dissent: A Safeguard of Democracy." *Journal of the American Judicature Society* 32: 104–7.

Edelman, Paul H., David E. Klein, and Stefanie A. Lindquist. 2012. "Consensus, Disorder, and Ideology on the Supreme Court." *Journal of Empirical Legal Studies* 9: 129–48.

Edwards, Linda H. 2010. *Legal Writing: Process, Analysis, and Organization.* Frederick, MD: Aspen.

Enquist, Ann, and Laurel Currie Oates. 2009. *Just Writing: Grammar, Punctuation, and Style for the Legal Writer.* New York: Aspen.

Epstein, Lee, and Jack Knight. 1998. *The Choices Justices Make.* Washington, DC: CQ Press.

Epstein, Lee, William M. Landes, and Richard A. Posner. 2011. "Why (and When) Judges Dissent: A Theoretical and Empirical Analysis." *Journal of Legal Analysis* 3: 101–37.

Epstein, Lee, and Jeffrey A. Segal. 2000. "Measuring Issue Salience." *American Journal of Political Science* 44: 66–83.

Epstein, Lee, Jeffrey A. Segal, and Harold J. Spaeth. 2001. "The Norm of Consensus on the U.S. Supreme Court." *American Journal of Political Science* 45: 362–77.

Epstein, Lee, Jeffrey A. Segal, Harold J. Spaeth, and Thomas G. Walker. 2007. *The Supreme Court Compendium: Data, Decisions, and Developments.* Washington, DC: CQ Press.

Faulkner, Stanley. 1958. "Review: *The Legacy of Holmes and Brandeis* by Samuel J. Konefsky." *Science & Society* 22: 174–77.

Federal Judicial Center. 1991. *Judicial Writing Manual.* Washington, DC: Federal Judicial Center.

Fife, Madelyn, Greg Goelzhauser, Kaylee B. Hodgson, and Nicole Vouvalis. 2017. "Concurring and Dissenting without Opinion." *Journal of Supreme Court History* 42, no. 2: 171–92.

Garner, Bryan A. 2001. *Legal Writing in Plain English.* Chicago: University of Chicago Press.

———. 2002. *The Elements of Legal Style.* New York: Oxford University Press.

———. 2010. "Interviews with United States Supreme Court Justices." *Scribes Journal of Legal Writing* 13: 1–182.

———. 2013. *The Redbook: A Manual on Legal Style.* St. Paul, MN: West Academic.

Gilligan, Thomas W., and Keith Krehbiel. 1989. "Asymmetric Information and Legislative Rules with a Heterogeneous Committee." *American Journal of Political Science* 33, no. 2: 459–90.

Ginsburg, Ruth Bader. 1990. "Remarks on Writing Separately." *Washington Law Review* 65: 133–50.

———. 2008. "Dissent Is an 'Appeal' for the Future." *Alaska Bar Rag* 32, no. 2: 1, 6.

———. 2010. "The Role of Dissenting Opinions." *Minnesota Law Review* 95: 1–8.

———. 2017. Interview with Tricia Johnson and Elliot Gerson. Aspen Institute. https://aspen-ideas-festival-production.s3.us-east-2.amazonaws.com/null1f0f2e49-bbc8-4dc2-abae-027172979cf7/V2AspenIdeasToGo_RBGrebroadcast.pdf [accessed February 2, 2022].

Goelzhauser, Greg. 2015. "Silent Acquiescence on the Supreme Court." *Justice System Journal* 36, no. 1: 3–19.

Goelzhauser, Greg, and Nicole Vouvalis. 2015. "Amicus Coalition Heterogeneity and Signaling Credibility in Supreme Court Agenda Setting." *Publius: The Journal of Federalism* 45, no. 1: 99–116.

Halpern, Stephen C., and Kenneth N. Vines. 1977. "Institutional Disunity, the Judges' Bill, and the Role of the U.S. Supreme Court." *Western Political Quarterly* 30: 471–83.

Hand, Learned. 1958. *The Bill of Rights.* Cambridge, MA: Harvard University Press.

Hansford, Thomas G., and James F. Spriggs II. 2006. *The Politics of Precedent on the U.S. Supreme Court.* Princeton, NJ: Princeton University Press.

Hausegger, Lori, and Lawrence Baum. 1999. "Inviting Congressional Action: A Study of Supreme Court Motivations in Statutory Interpretation." *American Journal of Political Science* 43, no. 1: 162–85.

Hendershot, Marcus E., Mark S. Hurwitz, Drew Noble Lanier, and Richard L. Pacelle Jr. 2013. "Dissensual Decision Making: Revisiting the Demise of Consensual Norms within the U.S. Supreme Court." *Political Research Quarterly* 66, no. 2: 467–81.

Hensley, Thomas R., and Scott P. Johnson. 1998. "Unanimity on the Rehnquist Court." *Akron Law Review* 31: 387–408.

Hettinger, Virginia A., Stefanie A. Lindquist, and Wendy L. Martinek. 2006. *Judging on a Collegial Court: Influences on Federal Appellate Decision Making.* Charlottesville: University of Virginia Press.

Hinkle, Rachael K., Morgan Hazelton, and Michael J. Nelson. 2017. "Legal Scholarship Highlight: Getting to Know You—The Unifying Effects of Membership Stability." *SCOTUSblog* (May 26, 2017, 12:11 PM), https://www.scotusblog.com/2017/05/legal -scholarship-highlight-getting-know-unifying-effects-membership-stability/.

Hinkle, Rachael K., and Michael J. Nelson. 2018. "How to Lose Cases and Influence People." *Statistics, Politics, and Policy* 8: 195–221.

Hughes, Charles Evans. 1928. *The Supreme Court of the United States: Its Foundation, Methods, and Achievements—An Interpretation.* New York: Columbia University Press.

Hume, Robert J. 2009. "The Impact of Judicial Opinion Language on Circuit Court Precedents." *Law & Society Review* 43: 127–50.

———. 2019. "Disagreeable Rhetoric, Shaming, and the Strategy of Dissenting on the U.S. Supreme Court." *Justice System Journal* 40: 3–20.

Hurwitz, Mark S., and Drew Lanier. 2004. "I Respectfully Dissent: Consensus, Agendas, and Policymaking on the U.S. Supreme Court, 1888–1999." *Review of Policy Research* 21: 429–45.

Jackson, Percival E. 1969. *Dissent in the Supreme Court: A Chronology.* Norman: University of Oklahoma Press.

Johnson, Timothy R., Ryan C. Black, and Eve M. Ringsmuth. 2008. "Hear Me Roar: What Provokes Supreme Court Justices to Dissent from the Bench." *Minnesota Law Review* 93: 1560.

Jordan, Kayla N., and James W. Pennebaker. 2016. "A Look into the First Clinton-Trump

Debate." Wordwatchers. https://wordwatchers.wordpress.com/2016/09/27/a-look
-into-the-first-clinton-trump-debate/ [accessed January 2, 2019].

Keck, Thomas M. 2004. *The Most Activist Supreme Court in History: The Road to Modern Judicial Conservatism.* Chicago: University of Chicago Press.

———. 2014. *Judicial Politics in Polarized Times.* Chicago: University of Chicago Press.

Kelman, Maurice. 1985. "The Forked Path of Dissent." *Supreme Court Review* 1985: 227–98.

Kelsh, John P. 1999. "The Opinion Delivery Practices of the United States Supreme Court 1790–1945." *Washington University Law Review* 77, no. 1: 137–82.

Kessler, Daniel, and Keith Krehbiel. 1996. "Dynamics of Cosponsorship." *American Political Science Review* 90, no. 3: 555–66.

Kilaru, Austin S., Jeanmarie Perrone, Catherine L. Auriemma, Frances S. Shofer, Frances K. Barg, and Zachary F. Meisel. 2014. "Evidence-Based Narratives to Improve Recall of Opioid Prescribing Guidelines: A Randomized Experiment." *Academic Emergency Medicine* 21: 244–49.

Kindy, Kimberly, Sari Horwitz, and William Wan. 2017. "Simply Stated, Gorsuch Is Steadfast and Surprising," *Washington Post,* February 18. https://www.washingtonpost.com/graphics/politics/gorsuch-profile/.

King, Gary, and Langche Zeng. 2001. "Explaining Rare Events in International Relations." *International Organization* 55, no. 3: 693–715.

Kluger, Richard. 1977. *Simple Justice.* New York: Vintage Books.

Kritzer, Herbert M., J. Mitchell Pickerill, and Mark Richards. 1998. "Bringing the Law Back In: Finding a Role for Law in Models of Supreme Court Decision-Making." Paper presented at the 1998 Annual Meeting of the Midwest Political Science Association, Chicago, April 23–25.

Larsen, Allison Orr. 2008. "Perpetual Dissents." *George Mason Law Review* 15: 447–78.

Lebovits, Gerald, Alifya V. Curtin, and Lisa Solomon. 2008. "Ethical Judicial Opinion Writing." *Georgetown Journal of Legal Ethics* 21: 237–309.

Leonhardt, David. 2000. "Word for Word: The Plain-Language Movement Hacking through the Thickets of Corporatespeak." *New York Times,* January 2. http://www.nytimes.com/2000/01/02weekinreview/word-for-word-plain-language-movement-hacking-through-thickets-corporatespeak.html.

Llewellyn, Karl N. 1934. "The Constitution as an Institution," *Columbia Law Review* 34: 1–40.

Long, Lance N., and William H. Christensen. 2008. "Clearly, Using Intensifiers Is Very Bad—or Is It?" *Idaho Law Review* 45: 171–89.

———. 2013. "When Justices (Subconsciously) Attack: The Theory of Argumentative Threat and the Supreme Court." *Oregon Law Review* 91: 933–59.

Maltzman, Forrest, James F. Spriggs II, and Paul J. Wahlbeck. 2000. *Crafting Law on the Supreme Court: The Collegial Game.* New York: Cambridge University Press.

Mar, Raymond A., Jingyuan Li, Anh T. P. Nguyen, and Cindy P. Ta. 2021. "Memory and Comprehension of Narrative versus Expository Texts: A Meta-Analysis." *Psychonomic Bulletin & Review* 28: 732–49.

Marcus, Maeva, ed. 2007. *The Documentary History of the Supreme Court of the United States, 1789–1800*. Vol. 8. New York: Columbia University Press.

Martin, Andrew D., and Kevin M. Quinn. 2002. "Dynamic Ideal Point Estimation via Markov Chain Monte Carlo for the U.S. Supreme Court, 1953–1999." *Political Analysis* 10: 134–53.

Mason, Alpheus Thomas. 1956. *Harlan Fiske Stone: Pillar of the Law*. New York: Viking Press.

Murphy, Walter F. 1964. *Elements of Judicial Strategy*. Chicago: University of Chicago Press.

O'Brien, David. 2017. *Storm Center: The Supreme Court in American Politics*. 11th ed. New York: Norton.

Osbeck, Mark. 2012. "What Is 'Good Legal Writing' and Why Does It Matter?" *Drexel Law Review* 4: 417–67.

Owens, Ryan J., and Justin Wedeking. 2011. "Justices and Legal Clarity: Analyzing the Complexity of U.S. Supreme Court Opinions." *Law & Society Review* 45, no. 4: 1027–61.

Owens, Ryan J., Justin Wedeking, and Patrick C. Wohlfarth. 2013. "How the Supreme Court Alters Opinion Language to Evade Congressional Review." *Journal of Law and Courts* 1: 35–59.

Parker, Carol McCrehan. 1997. "Writing Throughout the Curriculum: Why Law Schools Need It and How to Achieve It." *Nebraska Law Review* 76: 561–603.

Pennebaker, James W., R. L. Boyd, K. Jordan, and K. Blackburn. 2015. *The Development and Psychometric Properties of LIWC2015*. Austin, TX: University of Texas at Austin.

Pennebaker, James W., and Lori A. King. 1999. "Linguistic Styles: Language Use as an Individual Difference." *Journal of Personality and Social Psychology* 77, no. 6: 1296–312.

Peppers, Todd C., and Artemus Ward, eds. 2012. *In Chambers: Stories of Supreme Court Law Clerks and Their Justices*. Charlottesville: University of Virginia Press.

Perry, H. W. 1991. *Deciding to Decide: Agenda Setting in the United States Supreme Court*. Cambridge, MA: Harvard University Press.

Peterson, Steven A. 1981. "Dissent in American Courts." *Journal of Politics* 43: 412–34.

Pickerill, J. Mitchell. 2004. *Constitutional Deliberation in Congress: The Impact of Judicial Review in a Separated System*. Durham, NC: Duke University Press.

Post, Robert. 2001. "The Supreme Court Opinion as Institutional Practice: Dissent, Legal Scholarship, and Decisionmaking in the Taft Court." *Minnesota Law Review* 85: 1267–390.

Pound, Roscoe. 1922. *An Introduction to the Philosophy of Law*. New Haven, CT: Yale University Press.

Powell, Lewis F., Jr. Papers. Washington & Lee University, Lexington, VA.

Pritchett, C. Herman. 1941. "Divisions of Opinion among Justices of the U.S. Supreme Court, 1939–1941." *American Political Science Review* 35: 890–98.

———. 1945. "Dissent on the Supreme Court, 1943–44." *American Political Science Review* 39: 42–54.

————. 1948. *The Roosevelt Court*. New York: Macmillan.

Rehnquist, William H. 1973. "The Supreme Court: Past and Present." *American Bar Association Journal* 59: 361–64.

Romano, Michael K., and Todd A. Curry. 2019. *Creating the Law: State Supreme Court Opinions and the Effect of Audiences*. New York: Routledge.

Rosen, Jeffrey. 2007. "Robert's Rules." *Atlantic Monthly* 499: 104–13.

Rosenberg, Gerald N. 1991. *The Hollow Hope: Can Courts Bring About Social Change?* Chicago: University of Chicago Press.

Rotunda, Ronald D. 2017. "The Fall of Seriatim Opinions and the Rise of the Supreme Court." *Verdict*, October 9. https://verdict.justia.com/2017/10/09/fall-seriatim-opinions-supreme-court [accessed January 16, 2022].

Russell, Layne. 2000. *A Guide to Legal Analysis, Research, and Writing*. Lincoln, NE: iUniverse.com.

Sala, Brian R., and James F. Spriggs II. 2004. "Designing Tests of the Supreme Court and the Separation of Powers." *Political Research Quarterly* 57: 197–208.

Salamone, Michael F. 2014. "Judicial Consensus and Public Opinion: Conditional Response to Supreme Court Majority Size." *Political Research Quarterly* 67, no. 2: 320–34.

Scalia, Antonin. 1998. "Dissents." *OAH Magazine of History* 13, no. 1: 18–23.

Schiess, Wayne. 2017. "Using Intensifiers Is Literally a Crime." *Michigan Bar Journal* 96, no. 8: 48–51.

Segal, Jeffrey A., and Albert Cover. 1989. "Ideological Values and the Votes of U.S. Supreme Court Justices." *American Political Science Review* 83: 557–65.

Segal, Jeffrey A., and Harold J. Spaeth. 2002. *The Supreme Court and the Attitudinal Model Revisited*. New York: Cambridge University Press.

Senior, Jennifer. 2013. "In Conversation: Antonin Scalia." *New York*, October 4. http://nymag.com/news/features/antonin-scalia-2013-10/.

Shapiro, Martin. 1964. *Law and Politics in the Supreme Court: New Approaches to Political Jurisprudence*. New York: Free Press of Glencoe.

Silverstein, Gordon. 2009. *Law's Allure: How Law Shapes, Constrains, Saves, and Kills Politics*. New York: Cambridge University Press.

Smith, Kevin H. 2005. "The Jurisprudential Impact of *Brown v. Board of Education*." *North Dakota Law Review* 81: 115–43.

Smith, Michael R. 2008. *Advanced Legal Writing: Theories and Strategies in Persuasive Writing*. Austin, TX: Aspen.

Songer, Donald R. 1982. "Consensual and Nonconsensual Decisions in Unanimous Opinions of the United States Courts of Appeals." *American Journal of Political Science* 26: 225–39. Sowards, Adam. 2009. *The Environmental Justice: William O. Douglas and American Conservation*. Corvallis: Oregon State University Press.

Spaeth, Harold J., Lee Epstein, Andrew D. Martin, Jeffrey A. Segal, Theodore J. Ruger, and Sara C. Benesh. 2021. *2021 Supreme Court Database*, version 2021, release 01. http:\\Supremecourtdatabase.org.

Spaeth, Harold J., and Jeffrey A. Segal. 1999. *Majority Rule or Minority Will: Adherence to Precedent on the U.S. Supreme Court*. New York: Cambridge University Press.

Spriggs, James F. II. 1996. "The Supreme Court and Federal Administrative Agencies: A Resource-Based Theory and Analysis of Judicial Impact." *American Journal of Political Science* 40: 1122–51.

Spriggs, James F. II, and Thomas G. Hansford. 2001. "Explaining the Overruling of U.S. Supreme Court Precedent." *Journal of Politics* 63: 1091–111.

———. 2002. "The U.S. Supreme Court's Incorporation and Interpretation of Precedent." *Law & Society Review* 36: 139–60.

Stack, Kevin M. 1996. "The Practice of Dissent in the Supreme Court." *Yale Law Journal* 105: 2235–60.

Stevenson, Dwight W. 1975. "Writing Effective Opinions." *Judicature* 3: 134–39.

Stolberg, Sheryl Gay. 2009. "Obama Signs Equal-Pay Legislation." *New York Times,* January 29. https://www.nytimes.com/2009/01/30/us/politics/30ledbetter-web.html [accessed January 31, 2022].

Stone, Harlan F. 1942. "Dissenting Opinions Are Not without Value." *Journal of the American Judicature Society* 26: 78.

Strunk, William, Jr., and E. B. White. 1999. *The Elements of Style.* Needham Heights, MA: Allyn & Bacon.

Tausczik, Yla R., and James W. Pennebaker. 2010. "The Psychological Meaning of Words: LIWC and Computerized Text Analysis Methods." *Journal of Language and Social Psychology* 29, no. 1: 24–54.

Thompson, D. F. 2008. "Deliberative Democratic Theory and Empirical Political Science." *Annual Review of Political Science* 11: 497–520.

Thorndyke, Perry. 1979. "Knowledge Acquisition from Newspaper Stories." *Discourse Processes* 2: 95–112.

Ulmer, S. Sidney. 1970. "The Use of Power in the Supreme Court: The Opinion Assignments of Earl Warren, 1953–1960." *Journal of Public Law* 19, no. 1: 49–67.

Unah, Isaac, and Ange-Marie Hancock. 2006. "U.S. Supreme Court Decision Making, Case Salience, and the Attitudinal Model." *Law & Policy* 28: 295–320.

Urofsky, Melvin I. 2012. "Mr. Justice Brandeis and the Art of Judicial Dissent." *Pepperdine Law Review* 39, no. 4: 919–38.

———. 2017. *Dissent and the Supreme Court: Its Role in the Court's History and the Nation's Constitutional Dialogue.* New York: Vintage Books.

Van Dijk, Teun. 1983. "Discourse Analysis: Its Development and Application to the Structure of News." *Journal of Communication* 33: 20–43.

Vickrey, William C., Douglas G. Denton, and Hon. Wallace B. Jefferson. 2012. "Opinions as the Voice of the Court: How State Supreme Courts Can Communicate Effectively and Promote Procedural Fairness." *Court Review* 48, no. 3: 74–85.

Vinson, Fred M. 1949. "Supreme Court Work; Opinion on Dissents." *Journal of the Oklahoma Bar Association* 20: 1269–75.

Wahlbeck, Paul J. 2006. "Strategy and Constraints on Supreme Court Opinion Assignment." *University of Pennsylvania Law Review* 154: 1729–55.

Wahlbeck, Paul J., James F. Spriggs II, and Forrest Maltzman. 1999. "The Politics of Dissents and Concurrences on the U.S. Supreme Court." *American Politics Research* 27, no. 4: 488–514.

Walker, Thomas G., Lee Epstein, and William J. Dixon. 1988. "On the Mysterious Demise of Consensual Norms in the United States Supreme Court." *Journal of Politics* 50: 361–89.

Walsh, David J. 1997. "On the Meaning and Pattern of Legal Citations: Evidence from State Wrongful Discharge Precedent Cases." *Law & Society Review* 31: 337–62.

Ward, Artemus, and David L. Weiden. 2006. *Sorcerers' Apprentices: 100 Years of Law Clerks at the United States Supreme Court.* New York: NYU Press.

Warren, Charles. 1932. *The Supreme Court in United States History.* Vol. 1. Rev. ed. Boston: Little, Brown.

Way, Lori Beth, and Charles C. Turner. 2006. "Disagreement on the Rehnquist Court: The Dynamics of Supreme Court Concurrence." *American Politics Research* 34, no. 3: 293–318.

Williams, Joseph M. 2007. *Style Lessons in Clarity and Grace.* London: Pearson Education.

Wood, Sandra L., and Gary M. Gansle. 1997. "Seeking a Strategy: William J. Brennan's Dissent Assignments." *Judicature* 81: 73–75.

Zilis, Michael, and Justin Wedeking. 2020. "The Sources and Consequences of Political Rhetoric: Issue Importance, Collegial Bargaining, and Disagreeable Rhetoric in Supreme Court Opinions." *Journal of Law & Courts* 8, no. 2: 203–27.

Zink, James R., James F. Spriggs II, and John T. Scott. 2009. "Courting the Public: The Influence of Decision Attributes on Individuals' Views of Court Opinions." *Journal of Politics* 71, no. 3: 909–25.

Zinsser, William. 1980. *On Writing Well: An Informal Guide to Writing Nonfiction.* New York: Harper & Row.

ZoBell, Karl M. 1959. "Division of Opinion in the Supreme Court: A History of Judicial Disintegration." *Cornell Law Quarterly* 44: 186–221.

INDEX

Page numbers in *italics* refer to figures and tables.

Recent books in the series
CONSTITUTIONALISM AND DEMOCRACY

* 9 7 8 0 8 1 3 9 5 0 1 7 4 *